First Kiss

Lasting to Bliss

Hope & Inspiration
for Your Marriage

Lori D. Lowe

Published by Geode Publishing
9801 Fall Creek Rd., #133
Indianapolis, IN 46256

For information about the author or bulk purchases, please visit www.LoriDLowe.com.

Book designed by Sharron Wright, Dragonfly Design, Inc.

ISBN 978-0-984-04510-5

Printed in the United States of America.

CONTENTS

DEDICATION

This book is dedicated to the dozen brave and generous couples who opened their lives to me and shared how they found joy and love, sometimes in the bleakest of circumstances.

And to my wonderful husband, Ming, who has taught me what a blessing marriage can be, and who has given me the two best gifts in the world.

And to you, the reader: I wish you lasting marital bliss.

HUNTING FOR PERFECTION

Wading waist-deep down Missouri's Fox River on a hot summer day, I learned to hunt for geodes. These semi-round sedimentary rocks, said to be 350 million years old, contain hidden crystals. The casual hiker sees rocks, but geode hunters notice their cauliflower-shaped exterior and envision gem-like interiors.

At the sweet, shallow spot of "The Fox," abundant geodes range in size from a newborn's fist to more than 100 pounds, discovered under the water and lying nearby in the grass, as if tossed there during an Easter egg hunt for us to find. We also found them lodged in the riverbanks with ten feet of earth pressing down on them—half circles poking out of the earthen wall, waiting for erosion to release them into the river.

Geodes' sparkling interiors are generally white or clear, but some are colored, depending on mineral content. The product of a combination of water, natural chemicals, pressure, and heat, each porous geode is unique. There is no way to tell which will open to reveal a crystal treasure and which will reveal a solid mass or a greasy ball of sediment.

We're a lot like geodes, and so are our marriages. Without exception, we feel pressure from all sides, which can at times feel like the weight of the world. There is no shortage of muck dredged up in our society and no way to prevent seepage of this sediment into our lives. Some people, like geodes, use stressful situations to help shape, improve, and crystallize themselves. Others crumble under the pressure, store the muck for someone else to discover, or become hardened masses—of no real value to others.

For this book, I interviewed happily married couples across the country, some who have faced intense adversity—the kind that would pummel most marriages—yet became closer as a result. I tried to discover what made some marriages succeed despite hardship, while others wash away with the first storm. Successful couples don't just "overcome" adversity; instead, they become changed by it and incorporate what they have learned into a more perfect union.

We're all hunting for perfection—in ourselves, in others, and in our relationships. We won't find it by looking at the outer shell. Just as there isn't just one path for creating an ideal geode (volcanic geodes differ greatly in composition and form from Mexican "coconut" geodes, for example), there certainly isn't one recipe for an extraordinary marriage, although there are some common ingredients. Since we have different needs and personalities, no magic technique will work for all marriages. Still, despite our range of challenges, we humans share similar fears, desires, and longings. So when some couples uncover what makes a marriage—even one fraught with major obstacles—work well, we want to hear their story, to draw our own conclusions and to add them to our own life experiences. Success stories are all around us if we listen.

At some point, all marriages will face intense pressure. Will the pressure change you? Undoubtedly. Will it break you apart? Maybe. It may also create something entirely new and better than expected, like the twin-chambered geode, a merger of two hollow geodes. Learning how others have handled crises can help you prepare for your own.

Lest we think true love is a one-in-a-million find, consider that each spring, countless geodes are released from the earth, a seemingly impossible product of millions of years of time and energy. Be open to the possibility that your hunt for perfection is over, that your marriage is perfect but unfinished, being honed by outside forces, in the same way that a child is a perfect but incomplete person—no less perfect because he or she is in the early stages in life.

The couples profiled in this book are from different generations and walks of life, but they all became united in their difficulties. Those who faced multiple tests found their marriage became stronger with each one. Each couple found joy together, even amidst chaotic lives. These are not couples who merely "stuck it out"; theirs are great love stories whose commitment is not dependent on their circumstances. I hope they contribute to your own love story.

Lesson:

Never take your life, health or sobriety for granted.
Steer clear of addictions.

CHAPTER 1:

ADDICTED TO LOVE

The secrets to a great marriage, jokes Brian Jones* of Orlando, Florida, are "a short memory and selective hearing." Brian is kidding, but there's a hint of truth to his words—particularly the short memory part. A short memory would enable Brian and his wife, Melanie*, to forget some painful days in their past—like the day Melanie ordered Brian to leave their house after learning he was addicted to cocaine, or the day Melanie was diagnosed with aggressive breast cancer, three months after giving birth to their daughter. But they do remember these days, and both agree that their marriage is stronger today having lived through them.

Melanie and Brian got along well from the time they met. It was 1990, and both Brian and Melanie had recently relocated to Florida to start businesses of their own and enjoy a warmer climate. Neither was looking for a serious relationship, as both had broken off previous engagements. (Melanie had already received six marriage proposals and been engaged twice. Her most recent suitor had revealed his serious commitment issues the day after proposing to her by hyperventilating into a bag.) A couple of chance meetings at an indoor market, at which they had both set up booths, convinced Brian to invite Melanie to play tennis. They quickly developed a friendship. Melanie liked his quick smile (he smiles from his eyes), his sense of humor, and his goofiness. "He adds fun to life," she says. "We get each other's stupid jokes." Brian was attracted by her looks, but also her sense of patience and tolerance. He says she had a good sense of humor and seemed to like him.

Melanie and Brian were friends first. They enjoyed playing tennis and hanging out together. Brian, who was regularly fixed up with women by clients, even shared some of his date stories with Melanie—but after a while, she didn't want to hear them anymore, and she told him so. Suddenly, realizing that Melanie might be interested, Brian no longer wanted to be fixed up, but he was reluctant to date Melanie because he didn't want to lose her friendship. One day, over lunch, they talked about their dilemma, and both decided it was worth the risk. Something was different this time, they say. "We always had this really fun, great friendship," Melanie says, and they built on the relationship from there.

While they wanted to be together, both were a little nervous about the prospect of marriage. A conversation with Melanie's father helped them realize marriage is more of a decision than "knowing" whether someone is the perfect soul mate. "Marriage doesn't mean there aren't other people out there for you, or that you would never be attracted to anyone else," Brian says. "It's a decision that you want to be together." Six months into their relationship, a hypothetical discussion about marriage over homemade pizza turned into an impromptu wedding proposal. They excitedly became engaged and called their families with the good news. "I remember with the commitment of the engagement, the little bit of insecurity went away," Brian says. Melanie viewed marriage as a lifetime commitment. In Brian, she saw everything she wanted in a mate. Once she made the mental shift that she was ready, she didn't doubt her decision.

They were married in the fall of 1992, just over a year after meeting. The wedding took place outside, despite frost on the ground, on the banks of Boston's Charles River near Melanie's family's home. Melanie, then 29, had sold her half of her business to her partner, and Brian, then 33, did the same. Brian decided to work in real-estate development, and Melanie helped out by doing clerical work for his business. Their relationship was strong. A little over a year later, in the fall of 1993, they gave birth to a son, Lucas.

In the beginning, Brian traveled frequently, managing real-estate projects. Soon, the family moved temporarily to California, where Brian was managing a year-long on-site project. Melanie and Lucas, then an infant, returned home every couple of months to see family and friends, and moved back for good when the job was about six weeks from completion. Brian stayed in California until the project's end. It was during this period, when Brian had a lot of time on his own, that a troubled past, marked by drug use, started to catch up to him.

Losing His Way

During his youth, Brian avoided all kinds of drugs. The baby of the family, he was a little spoiled. "I had a great childhood," he concedes, although his parents didn't get along well. He got good grades and played tennis and soccer. "I was the smart jock. I was in the Honor Society. I didn't have to work too hard for anything. I was straight-laced and a little fearful." But when things got tougher in college, he started losing his way. He drank some during his college fraternity days and remembers trying marijuana at some point, "but I didn't like the feeling it gave me," he says. "I wasn't in control."

During graduate school, his routine had less structure—and Brian says he didn't have the self-discipline required to succeed. He wanted to go to medical school, but had to drop out of an accelerated course when it became too tough. He then switched to pre-law and did fairly well, but he was impatient, wanting to get out into the business world. He attributes the decision to leave grad school and move back home to Philadelphia to "immaturity, impatience, and a lack of direction." When his father—a CPA—asked Brian to join his accounting firm, he agreed. He got along well with his father, and sympathized with the fact that his father could never please his mother. "Mom was never satisfied with what she had or her lot in life," Brian says. Soon, Brian bought a three-bedroom house in a blue-collar neighborhood only a few miles from the office.

While Brian got along fine with his parents, his brother—the black sheep of the family, with a serious drug addiction—was not so lucky. He had dropped out of society, and his whereabouts were unknown; essentially, he had been disowned by the family. After years with no communication from him, the family finally resorted to hiring a private investigator in the hopes of learning whether he was alive (he was). Brian's cousin, who lived close by, also experimented with drugs. One day, this cousin invited Brian to hang out. For the cousin, "hanging out" also meant using cocaine, and he offered some to Brian.

Brian doesn't know why he decided to try it, but he did. He and his cousin smoked freebase cocaine. Although some research shows that smoking cocaine is harder on the liver and the lungs, it is nonetheless a popular way to ingest the drug because it is absorbed immediately into the blood, reaching the brain in seconds. In addition to leaving no telltale signs of drug use (unlike snorting or injecting), the rush from smoking cocaine is said to be more intense —although the high lasts only five to ten minutes.

Brian says that the first time he used cocaine, "I enjoyed it. It's not harsh. It wasn't an out-of-your mind high. It's just a nice feeling. Eventually, you chase the feeling and you go out of your mind, but that's long-term." Brian also liked that it made him feel in control. "Coke gave me a feeling of control that I liked." That first time was free, and Brian told himself that while he liked it, he would never pay for it himself. He was wrong, of course. "Did I ever pay for it," he says.

At first, Brian hid the occasional habit well, but eventually began using to the point that it affected his work and relationships (although one girlfriend, a woman 15 years his senior, started using with him). Living so close to the office, he regularly escaped to his house during the day to get his fix. "I hid it, and my parents didn't know or suspect even that I was with that crowd. They were gullible, and I was good at hiding. How they didn't know, I have no idea," he says. Then Brian got in deeper. "I was going on 24-hour binges. It was impossible for them not to realize at that point," he says. "I reached a point where I knew I had to stop."

Brian knew he needed a major life change. He went to an outpatient rehabilitation program in San Francisco, moving in with his best friend and college roommate. This friend, who was in the Bay Area studying for a Ph.D. and who later became a physician, proved a good influence and encouraged him to stay clean. Brian got a job selling cars and tried to start his life over. He stayed clean for a while, but "it didn't stick." Eventually, he started up again, hiding his drug use from his friend. After a few years in California, Brian felt drugs were again taking over his life, and he decided to move back home. A second stint in rehab—this time in Philadelphia—helped him get clean.

Once he was clean again, Brian continued working in car sales, then pursued other business ventures. Thinking it would give him another chance to be a doctor, he enrolled in podiatry school, but found it too difficult; he dropped out after just one semester. Again, he says he lacked self-discipline. After being in class eight hours a day, the last thing he wanted to do was spend another four hours in the evening studying.

He began dating a new woman seriously, and they became engaged—but the relationship reminded Brian of his parents' marriage, with lots of arguing and little happiness. Not surprisingly, he again found himself drawn to cocaine. When his fiancée found out that he'd lapsed, "I promised I would never use again, and she forgave me." Even so, they broke up—although not because of Brian's drug use. "It was kind of an addictive relationship," he explains, with frequent splits and reconciliations. Brian felt he needed to get away, and decided to move to Florida. "She wanted to follow me, but I decided it would have been like my parents' marriage," he says.

Brian and a friend from rehab in Philadelphia decided to start a clothing business in Florida. After all he had been through, he was looking more at getting his life on track than falling in love—but that's when he met Melanie. Before getting too serious, Brian told Melanie that "he had used drugs in the past, got in too heavy, and stopped when it became a problem," Melanie, who herself had experimented with marijuana in her younger days, explains. "I may not have been forthcoming with all the details," Brian says. They didn't discuss the types of drugs he had used or other details. "As long as it's in the past," she said. She didn't ask many questions. "It never occurred to me that he had a serious addiction," Melanie says. She did warn Brian, however, that she would leave him if he ever returned to drugs; after that, the topic was put to rest.

According to Brian, drug users develop a kind of sixth sense about who has drugs or has used drugs. When he worked in car sales or construction, he'd get to know some of the guys, their families, and intimate details of their lives. A comment would be made, and he'd ask a question. It would come out that he had cocaine or dealt the drug. "I never went on a street corner in a bad section of town to get it. It was always someone I had worked with," explains Brian. And that's how it happened when Brian was in California, working that development job, with his family back in Florida. A contractor who was putting in a concrete patio said something in conversation. "It piqued my interest. It turns out he dealt (cocaine). I had no idea it would come up," Brian says. So Brian bought some. "Why did I? I never learned my lesson, and I thought I could get away with it," Brian says. "I wasn't miserable in my marriage. If I thought it was going to affect my life and I might lose my wife and child, I wouldn't have," he says. He says he thought "this time would be different."

"Throughout my life, I never learned about cause and effect—consequential thinking," Brian says, "For example, if you want something, you have to work for it." He also says he was slow to grow up. "Some of us grow up in our 20s or 30s, some in our 40s. Some of us never grow up." Brian always maintained a sense of self worth, though—something his brother had lost. He realizes now that his thinking was faulty. "I will destroy myself with drugs and ruin everything that I love, but I was maintaining that I had a sense of self worth. It's kind of contradictory," he says. He also seemed to differentiate between the refined cocaine used recreationally by professional types and crack cocaine, sold on the streets.

For quite a while, Brian used drugs only occasionally—once a month, if that. He could use them and put them aside. Eventually, however, his use increased. By this time, he was back in Florida, living with his family. "I remember going golfing early in the morning for a 7 o'clock tee time. I'd come back at 11:30, and I'd be so excited if (Melanie) wasn't there and had her own plans so I could do it," Brian says. Even if she was home, he learned to hide his habit exceedingly well. "She'd be downstairs. I'd take a hit in a closet and then come down and see her. It was unbelievable how well I hid it," he says. Brian remembers telling Melanie he would meet her at all their events—his son's preschool play, a friend's Bar Mitzvah—so he could get high just before. He says Melanie was naïve and trusting—not ignorant, just unsuspecting. Melanie explains that there was no smell of any kind or lingering smoke. "Apparently, it's a clean burn. You see nothing. There are no telltale signs around. There's no evidence. It takes only seconds." She adds that he never seemed impaired to her. Looking back, Melanie says the only early symptoms she saw were excessive sweating, an occasional cough, and frequent lateness, along with certain personality changes.

Melanie knew, however, that something was wrong. At first, she figured Brian was just busy juggling all his responsibilities. Then she thought he might be sick because of his cough, or depressed or bipolar because of his personality change. By the time their son was four years old, Brian had become more irritable and wasn't sleeping much. He was always late and on edge. He wasn't the man she married, and she became increasingly concerned. She asked him repeatedly what was going on. He'd say, "I don't know" or "I don't feel right" and agree to anything she suggested.

They attended couples therapy for months; he even agreed to take an antidepressant. "He said, 'I'll do anything you want. Just don't leave,'" Melanie says. As part of an evaluation, the therapist asked him if he was using any kind of drugs, and he said no. (Brian wonders now if he was trying to fool the therapist or if he was trying to convince himself he didn't have a drug problem.) Melanie says she talked to the therapist later, and the therapist didn't think he exhibited any of the traits of a drug addict. If a trained therapist didn't see the signs, how could Melanie?

They argued constantly; Melanie, who was seriously considering leaving, felt Brian just wouldn't "fess up" to what was going on. But Brian thought Melanie would leave him if he was honest about the drug use. "It became a vicious cycle," he says. The drug use was creating financial and marital problems, and he was using the drugs to escape his problems. "First it's enjoyable, but it makes things worse. It's immediate gratification," Brian says.

Coming Clean, Getting Clean

One night, Brian stayed out until 3 a.m.; Melanie waited up for him. When he came in, "I was screaming and coming unglued," she says. "He looked wild-eyed." In that moment, he knew Melanie would leave if he didn't do something. He told her, "I need to tell you what's going on, but I just can't right now. I need to get a few hours of sleep," Melanie recalls. She told him, "I don't know what this is, but you need to tell me today, or we're done."

After Brian went to sleep, Melanie and Lucas went to a friend's house. By then, all their friends knew that Brian was acting "weird" and were equally stumped as to the reason. Around noon, Brian called and said he wanted to see her. He was ready to talk. Leaving Lucas outside in her friend's care, Melanie and Brian went inside her friend's house to talk. She said, "I'm here. I'm quiet. I'm listening. What's going on?"

Although Brian has difficulty remembering the conversation—he was still on drugs at the time—he recalls being very nervous. According to Melanie, Brian asked her, "What's the one thing you'd leave me for?" She said, "I don't know. Are you having an affair?" He said he wasn't. It was nothing like that. Frustrated, Melanie asked, "What?!" Finally, Brian said, "Drugs. I got into drugs. I'm so sorry. I don't know how I got into it." Melanie was stunned. "What are you talking about?" she asked him. "What kind of drugs?" Brian told her it was coke. She was shocked. "You're snorting coke?" she asked him. "No, I smoke it. I got caught up and I'm addicted now," he said. Melanie, looking out the window at her son playing in the driveway with her friend, became very angry. How could Brian put her and Lucas in this position? She responded quickly. "Get out. Take your stuff and get out now. When I come home in an hour, I want you gone," she said. "You jeopardized our child's life. You're using drugs with a child in the house. I don't know anything about what you're using or how it works, but I need you to be away from us instantly. I'm not kidding."

Brian went home. He packed a suitcase full of clothing and five photos and went to stay with a buddy. He knew there was a very good chance that Melanie would never take him back. Melanie sat with her friend in shock. Less than two hours later, she returned home with knots in her stomach, not sure if she would be more upset to find him at home or to *not* find him there. The house was empty. Melanie told Lucas his Daddy had to go out of town on business and waited for him to fall asleep; then she lay awake and cried for hours, "licking my wounds."

Two days later, Brian called with more devastating news. "He said, 'There's more. I spent a lot of money.'" He had depleted their savings and emergency accounts and had opened credit lines in his name, keeping the bills and statements from her. All told, Brian had spent approximately $100,000 in about two years. The pit in Melanie's stomach grew larger by the minute. She immediately feared they would lose their house. Brian tried to settle her fears. "I'm going into rehab," he said. "I'm going to fix it." But she was too angry. "I don't even want to hear what you do," she told him, adding that he would immediately lose control of all their assets. "I don't know how you're going to fix this or if I ever want to see you again, but I'm not letting you take me down," Melanie said. She warned Brian, "You will not see our child unless you fix yourself."

Immediately, Melanie took Brian's name off of a small checking account she had. She set about getting their finances in order and called both sets of their parents. Her parents, who loved Brian dearly, were astonished and angry. Her Dad said he would never speak to Brian again. Brian's own parents responded even more negatively than her own. "They were so upset because they knew about his drug history and what happened with his brother." They told Melanie they would not help Brian on any level, nor would they talk to him. They tried to be there for Melanie emotionally, but felt Brian would have to fix the mess he created himself.

Even after Melanie threw him out, Brian wasn't ready to stop using drugs. "I wasn't ready to be done," he says. He wanted to quit, but he wanted it to be on his terms, when he was ready. The addiction had a strong hold on him, and since he was still in possession of the drug, he felt the need to use, partly to escape the pain he had just caused his family. For a few days—he can't remember exactly how many—he camped out at the home of a friend's mother, who was on vacation. There, he used up the rest of his drug supply, and finally hit bottom. "I was so low," he says. "I reached a point where probably if I had more (cocaine), I may not have stopped." He adds, "One of the things I was actually grateful for is that I wasn't independently wealthy. Eventually, I would run out (of drugs) and financially it would not be feasible to buy more. That was a help for me." Finally, Brian understood that he had to make a permanent change and to try to make amends for the pain he caused others.

Brian moved in with his former business partner—the one he had met in rehab in Philadelphia—with whom he had remained friends. "He and his wife were there for me," Brian says. At the same time, Brian began a daily outpatient rehab program and frequently attended Alcoholics Anonymous (AA) meetings. Although he had completed AA's 12-step program before, he was more motivated this time. Brian also saw a therapist during this period. This lasted for about six months. "That seemed like years," he says. During that time, he says, "I had no idea if I would ever get Melanie back. I do remember getting rid of all expectations and doing what I had to do. I thought, 'What's meant to be will be.'"

But Melanie remained very angry. It wasn't just Brian's lies and deceit; seeing their son so sad about his daddy's absence broke her heart. "I tried to explain, on a four-year-old level, that Daddy made some mistakes and he has to fix them before he can come back." After Brian had been gone a few weeks, Lucas, crying, looked at her and begged, "Just let him come home!" Melanie says, "It made me hate Brian even more for doing this to me and to our child. This was not the plan (for our lives)."

In time, Brian called and said he needed to see Lucas. Melanie knew Lucas needed to see his father, but before she would allow it, she called around to verify that Brian was in a rehab program and was staying clean. Satisfied that Lucas would be safe with his father, she began allowing Brian to visit Lucas for one hour, twice a week, in her home. Melanie was torn. If she tried staying home during Brian's visits, inevitably her anger boiled to the surface and she found herself screaming at him. "It was ugly and horrible. We would scream at each other," Melanie says. "I remember one day even after he left and the garage door was closed, I was still screaming. It was so intense." But if she left, Lucas often cried. Eventually, though, Lucas got used to spending time with his dad alone.

Once he was off drugs and able to work, Brian took a job waiting tables. "It was very humbling," he says. He continued attending AA meetings, and always made his visits home. A couple of months went by. He wrote letters to Melanie and apologized repeatedly. "He made it so evident from day one that he took ownership of it. He'd say, 'I'm beyond screwing up,' and said he'd do everything in his power to fix this. When he did what he needed to do, it took some of the anger away," Melanie says. Brian says he wasn't being apologetic and humble just to get her back. He accepted that things might or might not work out. "But did I want it? Yeah. Did I cry and write about what I'd lost? Sure. Was I emotional? Sure."

Brian felt he had better success getting well this last time due to a combination of many factors. "I got a lot out of the meetings and the peer support from my friend, who attended with me. The outpatient program helped a lot. And, maybe the timing was right. It was a culmination of everything I learned over the years. One built on the other. I finally learned cause and effect." Brian recalls how his friend in San Francisco had been amazed that he could claw himself out of each hole and get his life back in order, but says when he reached that certain level of order, he got complacent, and "eventually (drugs) got me again." But after getting clean and well this time, Brian didn't get complacent, nor does he think he can ever use drugs again and remain in control. "I think I will always have this (addiction) problem. If I were to start using again, history would repeat itself. As much as I'd like to and still have fond memories of doing it, it's a tradeoff. It's life or that."

Seeking Forgiveness and a Fresh Start

Melanie knew Brian's drug use wasn't a personal attack on her. "On a rational level, I also knew that the person I married and the relationship we had (when he wasn't using) was still there." She says under all the problems, she knew love remained—although it was buried for a while. Slowly, the two started to talk on the phone. In time, they enjoyed a laugh here or there. "And then eventually, when he would see Lucas, I wouldn't leave right away." She watched him "do what needed to be done," including attending daily meetings. They had lunch occasionally and began to talk. "He said our family was the most important thing in the world to him," and he felt horrible that he had failed them. After six months of Brian working every day to "win the trust back," she agreed to go out on a date with him for New Year's. Then they went to dinner and a movie as a family. Soon, Brian asked if he could come back home so they could live as a family again. Melanie said, "I don't know how easy or hard that will be, but I'm willing to try." Melanie saw a changed man. "People make mistakes in life. Hopefully, they're not irreparable."

Throughout it all, Brian and Melanie had shared their problems with family and friends. "I wanted everyone there to catch him if, God forbid, he were to fall," Melanie says. After they reconciled, all four parents were able to forgive Brian, if somewhat reluctantly at first. "My Dad probably took a couple of years to look him in the eyes and hug him again," Melanie says. "I'm his only daughter, and he was probably thinking, 'How could you do this to her?' He couldn't comprehend (the drug use) on any level." Melanie says her Mom was very loving and saw that Brian was trying.

As for Brian, he saw forgiveness coming from family and friends well before he felt he deserved it. "It was pretty quick considering the magnitude of what I did. It's pretty amazing that we got back on track that quickly."He felt that was especially true of his wife's ability to forgive him. "That's a reflection on (her). It's what attracted me to her in the first place. She's tolerant and patient in all respects. She loves me for who I am with my flaws." Brian is still amazed that Melanie's mom, dad, and brother accepted him back into the family. "I know it was slow, but it seemed like it was in a moment once I was better," Brian says. "I remember being on the front lawn apologizing to (Melanie's) Mom. She was very matter of fact. She said, 'We all make mistakes. You're not a bad person.' It was accepting and pretty amazing." He admits that he doesn't know if he would have been as forgiving.

Financially, they were able to consolidate their debt and remortgage their house. Initially, Melanie took his name off of every account, which Brian agreed to. She managed the money, and Brian would have "a couple hundred dollars to his name." However, she says, "He's done nothing but handle it the right way and truthfully since then." She says if he hadn't, she would not have stayed with him. "I needed to know he was 100-percent on board. That made it easy for me to give back." (She still maintains a separate checking account, having vowed to never allow herself to be placed in such a vulnerable position.)

While Melanie, Brian, and Lucas were thrilled to be reunited as a family, Melanie and Brian decided to hold off on having additional children, at least for a while, and "love the one we had." But Melanie, who had always been close with her brother, wanted her son to have a sibling. "We waited years to make sure he could stay clean," Melanie says, but eventually they felt comfortable enough to have another child, a girl, when Lucas was six and a half years old. "Brian has always been a super dad," Melanie says. "He just loves the kids, and they know and feel that. He's very active and involved. They play tennis, go to the movies or watch chick flicks. He's very open with his emotions."

When Lucas was 10, Brian and Melanie told him about Brian's history with drug addiction. They wanted him to understand how horrible the drugs were and how it almost destroyed their family so that he would never want to experiment with them. "He sat there and cried and was blown away. He was devastated, but they talked about it, and (Brian) has always made him feel secure and loved," Melanie says.

Brian says during the 20-year period of on-again, off-again drug use, it was a stagnating period, financially and personally. "If I look at my tax returns from when I graduated college up to the point when I stopped (drugs), there were no accomplishments. Since then, that's all there have been," he says. "But at the same time, I feel everything I went through makes me who I am. I can't say I don't regret it. If I could go back again and do things differently, yes (I would), but at the same time, I have my wife and two kids. This is my life and this is all I really want. I may not have had it this way if I didn't go through what I did," Brian says.

A Second Test

Three months after Brian and Melanie's daughter was born, Melanie made a decision that would ultimately save her life. Unhappy with her breasts, she decided to undergo a breast reduction. Brian was not in favor of any cosmetic surgery—he loved her the way she was and saw the risks associated with the surgery—but he supported her decision. "If she really wants to do something I will support her, but it was not something I encouraged."

Before scheduling surgery, Melanie's surgeon required that Melanie, then 36, get a mammogram. After completing the procedure, Melanie was called in for a second mammogram "because they didn't get a good picture" on the first one. A few days later, the office requested that Melanie return for a needle biopsy, although they assured her she probably just had a cyst. Each time, Melanie told herself it probably had something to do with having recently given birth, and promptly took time off work (by then, she was working as a vice president of development for a commercial real-estate firm) to have the needed procedure done. When the doctor's office called again to request a core biopsy, Melanie realized something might be seriously wrong, despite her having no family history of breast cancer.

The core biopsy was somewhat painful, and she had to wait another week for the results, which she called "inhumane." She couldn't help thinking of her former business partner, who had recently died from cancer, diagnosed when her child, like Melanie's daughter, was only four months old. After what felt like an eternity, Melanie's physician's office called and requested that she come in for the results. She said, "If everything is fine, someone should tell me over the phone." They responded that they were not at liberty to give the results. Melanie hung up the phone and turned white. She called Brian and blurted out, "I think I have breast cancer."

The two met at the doctor's office to speak to the physician, whom Melanie had never met. "I remember staring at the floor, waiting and thinking, 'I just need to get through this.'" The physician walked in, shook their hands, and informed her of her diagnosis in the worst possible way. "Well, the thing you don't want to hear you are going to hear. You have breast cancer." Melanie gasped, and the doctor continued. "You have two choices, a single or double mastectomy." Melanie was appalled at his lack of grace or concern or even educational information. He said she could get a second opinion if she liked, and she said she would like one. That was the end of the meeting; she knew she never wanted to see that doctor again.

She didn't cry; she was shocked. "I remember Brian hugging me and telling me we'll get through this." Brian says he doesn't remember thinking Melanie could die. "I never recall breaking down or thinking this is the end of our world. I recall thinking we're going to have to deal with it, and we did. Part of me is pretty pragmatic," he says. "Most things we worry about don't come to pass." He does say, however, that he thought about what he could lose, and it made him more appreciative.

A friend's mother, who had connections on a hospital board, pulled some strings to get Melanie an appointment the very next day. To find out whether the cancer had metastasized, she underwent a full-body scan. After being injected with radioactive dye, Melanie was instructed to remain still for an hour. Melanie, who hadn't even considered the possibility of the cancer metastasizing, was very fearful, thinking again of her friend who had died from the disease. "The most horrific thoughts go through your mind," she says. Thankfully, the scan was clear; the cancer had not spread from her breast. The same friend's mother put Melanie in touch with a female breast surgeon, who fit Melanie in right away. Melanie asked the surgeon, "If this was you and your breast, what would you do?" The surgeon recommended a lumpectomy along with lymph-node removal to be sure the cancer hadn't spread, followed by chemotherapy and radiation. Melanie was thrilled she wouldn't have to undergo a mastectomy and scheduled her surgery for two weeks later.

The oncology surgeon worked in conjunction with a breast-reconstruction surgeon, enabling Melanie to obtain a breast reduction at the same time—all with minimal scarring. In fact, surgeons used the same incision for the reduction, the removal of 12 lymph nodes, and the removal of the tumor, which was two-centimeters of solid tissue with a very aggressive genetic makeup. "If I had waited another month," says Melanie, "I would probably be dead. It probably would have spread."

After taking a week off of work to recover from surgery, Melanie began six months of chemotherapy and radiation. Melanie had forewarned Lucas, then six years old, that she would lose her hair. She didn't tell him about the cancer; instead, she told him she had some "really bad germs" and that the doctors would give her some "really strong medicine" to make her feel better. She added, "The weird thing is that it's gonna make my hair fall out." Lucas asked what she would wear on her head. She told him they would go to the store and pick out a baseball hat. He asked, "What if it's a windy day, and it blows off?" Melanie told him, "Then we'll run down the street together and chase it, and we'll put it right back on my head." Lucas was amused by the story and comforted by the explanation. Melanie says she never let her son see how sick she got and didn't show him her bald head. She wore a wig in public and a bandana at home.

The fact was, Melanie was so ill that some days it took great effort to eat a piece of toast, and she frequently vomited. She took to driving back and forth to the office (about an hour each way) with a gallon-sized Ziploc bag in her lap, just in case she became sick. Melanie's mother, who had relocated to be near Melanie and Brian, took care of the baby many evenings, and a part-time nanny helped during the day. She says her husband was "nothing but supportive" and he kept the kids happy. "He was entirely there for me. We've been there for each other through good, bad, ugly and sick," Melanie says. She adds that Brian never once complained to anyone that his wife was sick. "He had a lot on his plate, but he just did what needed to be done." If she just needed someone to sit next to her, he would do that. He would ask, "What can I do? Do you want me to rub your back, or not touch you?" He would make her a baked potato or bring her some crackers, foods that she kept down better than others. Brian says Melanie was very strong during her illness and kept him from feeling overwhelmed. He saw her taking care of children, even when she was ill. He says although she was in a lot of pain, she kept it to herself.

Eight months after her diagnosis, around the time their daughter celebrated her first birthday, Melanie was considered cancer-free. Melanie returned to her doctor every three months, then every six to nine months, for blood work. When she reached the five-year mark, she was thrilled to get a clean bill of health and a good prognosis. She now has annual checkups and only a slightly increased chance of a recurrence compared with the general population. Each time she sees the results are clean, she breathes a sigh of relief.

Brian and Melanie both celebrate being "clean" for different reasons. "All we have is today," Brian says. "We don't know if we will get hit by a bus tomorrow or live to be 100. None of us are guaranteed anything." He adds that he is very thankful that she has had a full recovery, "but I don't want to jinx it."

Their Life Today

After 19 years of being married, Brian says his and Melanie's marriage is forever evolving and changing. He describes it as healthy, not perfect, growing, and having ups and downs. "But with all that, I still often stop and think I'm amazed she still loves me and wants to be with me as much as I want to be with her." He says marriage is a conscious decision that you're with the person you chose. Melanie says Brian, who travels frequently for work, writes love notes to her, sometimes leaving one on her pillow, but often sending them through the mail. He also leaves notes for the kids. He and the kids send pictures and e-mails back and forth. "He tries—we both do. To keep a really good relationship, you've got to try. It needs nurturing."

They schedule alone time, especially on the weekends, going for bike rides together or taking trips to the dog park. They also enjoy playing music and relaxing in the yard, or playing Backgammon or Scrabble. When the kids go to overnight summer camp, they take mini road tips to explore new places. Trying new things together keeps their relationship fresh, Melanie says.

They also look for ways to please one another. "A lot of little things really please her," Brian says. "It may take her a month to eat a chocolate cake; she'll eat a little bit at a time. I will finish the whole thing in 10 minutes." "We've learned the little things we can do make a difference, like saying something nice in an e-mail. It's nothing extraordinary like leaving a trail of petals to the bedroom filled with a thousand candles. We let each other know we're thinking of the other and that we really care," says Brian.

Melanie says they don't stay together just because of what they went through together; "We are just appreciative human beings." When Brian sees Melanie being thoughtful, it makes him want to be that way. However, they do agree that their marriage is strong today because of what they went through. Indeed, friends and acquaintances tell them they seem to have a strong marriage and say they'd like to have a marriage like theirs. Many of their friends have divorced. Melanie says it's easy to spot the negative couples when they go out; they're the ones making snide comments, acting unkindly, and lacking warmth in their conversations with one another. "If you don't build up your own spouse, who is going to?" she asks. Melanie and Brian go out of their way to compliment one another, privately and publicly. They also try to thank one another for things they do. "People need to feel appreciated," she says. "If you do your best to keep negative feelings out, and keep security, love, and warmth there on an ongoing basis, then when you do have negative feelings, you can come back from it," Melanie says. Brian says they have learned to build one another up. He adds that Melanie has taught him to be patient and accepting. They've also learned that anything worthwhile—be it one's health or sobriety or one's marriage—takes constant maintenance and effort.

Because he finally learned that his actions have consequences, Brian and Melanie try very hard to instill that lesson in their children. For instance, he tells them if they never try drugs, they can't get addicted, and if they drive too fast, they might get hurt. "We want it to hit home with our kids," he says, adding that he cannot control their choices.

Melanie says she loves Brian so much more than she did when they were first married, because now they have history and experience to boot. "It's a whole different level of love. Our bond is stronger than ever now." What makes their life exciting, Brian says, is a combination of both of them making a conscious effort to please the other person. They have experienced "ebbs and flows," but when they get in a rut, they discuss it, and try to be more affectionate or make some other needed change. "Often it's just the awareness and willingness to work that is enough," Brian says. "We both want to be healthy together and be in a positive relationship. She's the one I want to be with. I'm the one she wants to be with. We're very lucky."

The names of this couple were changed for professional reasons.

Lesson:

Focus on your strengths, not your sorrows.

CHAPTER 2:

CYCLING THROUGH LOVE AND LOSS

Not every couple who faces extreme trials will come to a breaking point. Some will use the experiences of intense pain to strengthen their bond, like the torch used to solder copper pipes together in a process called "sweating." The Johnsons are an example of a well-bonded couple whose relationship may be the envy of others. Before envying their bond, consider the sweat and tears that brought them to this ultimately happy place, and ask yourself if you could withstand such a process. When they met as teenagers, they certainly didn't anticipate the path their marriage would take.

A Rude Awakening

At about 5:30 a.m. on August 12, 2008, 38-year-old Robbie Johnson and his friend, Stuart, set out on one of their frequent long-distance bicycle rides. It was a little darker than they would have liked, but the sun was on its way up. Because Stuart was worried that riding on the hills around their Jonesboro, Arkansas, home would aggravate a recent wrist injury, the two men opted to ride about 30 miles along a flat, wide, five-lane highway they had ridden "hundreds of times" before. The men were careful to ride on the white line near the shoulder. As they pedaled, Stuart commented that it was a nice day for August, a little cooler than normal. As Robbie started to respond, he suddenly felt himself tumbling, spinning, flipping.

Robbie landed in a ditch near the grass, and Stuart dismounted and ran to his side. "What happened?" Robbie asked. Stuart explained that a truck had clipped him. "The truck driver stopped; he was very apologetic. He may have been texting or drinking coffee— we don't know," Robbie says. Several other drivers stopped to assist. "I tried to move a little, and everyone told me to stay still. I didn't sense how badly I was hurt," Robbie says. Stuart borrowed someone's phone and quickly called 911. He also called Robbie's wife, Stacey, to tell her Robbie had been hit. He explained that they were waiting for an ambulance, and that she should meet them at the hospital, just a few blocks from their home. Stacey called her father to come stay with their three children, who were still asleep; when he arrived, Stacey threw on some shorts, a t-shirt, and a baseball cap, and rushed out the door. She was quickly joined at the ER by her mother and Robbie's mother.

Once at the hospital, Robbie remained conscious, but was in shock. It wasn't until doctors placed him on a flat surface for an MRI and CT scan that Robbie experienced excruciating pain. "I knew it was not good," he says. When the pain spiked, Robbie briefly wondered whether he would survive, and naturally grew concerned about his wife and kids, but thanks to the drugs he'd been given and his generally optimistic nature, he believed he would pull through. Initially, doctors thought he had an open book pelvic fracture, placing him at high risk of bleeding out within about five hours, but that proved to be a misdiagnosis. Among other injuries, Robbie had a broken hip, a broken back, and a broken foot. He also had a large wound on his back that was causing significant blood loss.

Thankfully, his helmet, which had cracked from the impact, protected him from any brain injuries.

Robbie's doctors realized that they needed to quickly transport Robbie to a trauma center to control his heavy bleeding. They contacted a trauma center in Memphis, but it was full. Then they tried to send him to one in Little Rock, but a storm prevented successful transport. They called a hospital in Cape Girardeau, Missouri, but there were no trauma surgeons available. As the ER team made their way down the list of trauma centers, several of Robbie's physician friends, whom Robbie knew from his work in the pharmaceutical industry and also from church, crowded into the ER. One helped put his hip back in place to restore blood flow; another took care of his bleeding.

"It was looking really bad at one point," Stacey says. "I asked the doctor (about his prognosis), and he said, 'We've got to get your husband out of here,' and explained his injuries to me. I asked him, 'Are you telling me my husband might die?' He said, "Yes, I'm telling you he might die." Devastated by this news, Stacey retreated to a corner of the waiting room. "I needed to get my wits about me," she explains. She agonized over how she could live without Robbie, her best friend. She prayed, "Please, don't ask me to give him up. I'm a 37-year-old mother with three children. Please, don't ask me to raise them alone." And of course, she remembered the raw grief she had felt when she had lost her baby daughter, Abigail, 10 years before. "I asked God to please not ask this of me again."

Abby's Impact

Abby was born in March of 1998, the younger sister to healthy big-brother, Nathan. Although Stacey had carried Abby to term, Abby weighed in at a mere 4 pounds, 11 ounces, and was pale and bluish at birth. "The doctors put her on oxygen and were having trouble pinking her up," Stacey says. "They also didn't understand why she was so tiny and frail. She didn't cry immediately." Shortly after her birth mid-afternoon, Abby was given an echocardiogram. By 5:30 that evening, she was on a helicopter to Children's Hospital in Little Rock—where, incidentally, Stacey's brother, who was in medical school, lived—diagnosed with a heart defect. Physicians explained to Stacey and Robbie that Abby's aorta and pulmonary arteries were transposed, a condition that causes too much blood to flow to the lungs and not enough to flow to the extremities. She also had a small hole in her heart (although this turned out to be a blessing, because it allowed some oxygenation of her blood and kept her heart beating long enough to get her to Little Rock). The pediatric specialists at Children's, however, were reluctant to perform surgery on such a small infant. (Usually, heart defects are found on full-size babies or children.) They wanted to postpone surgery as long as possible while Abby grew in size.

"Once we got her checked in and talked to the cardiologist, then went to [Stacey's brother's] house, I remember just breaking down," Robbie says. "To me, this was the death of a dream. Financially, we were a young married couple. We have a child who is profoundly ill, and we may have medical bills for the rest of our lives." Robbie was overwhelmed by other feelings as well. "I've always wanted a girl. We loved the name Abigail. She was going to be Daddy's little girl. Walking her down the aisle and all the dreams that may never happen, they just downpoured." For her part, Stacey, who had been discharged from the hospital just six hours after giving birth so she could travel to Little Rock with her daughter, felt numb. "I was emotional and sad and of course crying, but I kicked into 'Mom has got to take care of things' mode." Stacey's mother came to help, and Robbie's parents took care of their son, Nathan. Stacey called her father, who was traveling in Rome, and advised him to come home, since they didn't know if Abby would survive.

The next day, Robbie and Stacey felt renewed hope. They saw all the babies in the NICU and the excellent nursing care provided. The doctors also gave them hope. Their pastor came to visit. They saw their pastor again that night—this time on the evening news program, *Nightline*, with Ted Koppel. The day after Abby's birth, Jonesboro had become the focus of national attention when two middle-school students shot and killed a teacher and four students and injured 10 others. The incident occurred at Westside Middle School, where Stacey's father had been a teacher, administrator, and coach. The teacher who was killed was a family friend. Stacey's father learned of the news during a layover on his trip home. Needless to say, for the Johnsons, the days surrounding Abby's birth and the shooting seemed surreal.

Abby improved in the NICU at Children's, and after about a week, she was discharged. Back home, friends helped by moving the Johnson family's belongings into their new home and unpacking for them. (Robbie and Stacey had been in the process of moving when Abby was born but were only halfway done.) Relieved their ordeal was over, Robbie and Stacey drove their baby girl the two hours home. "Doctors told us to watch for little beads of sweat on her forehead to show she was working too hard," Stacey says. "We would fortify the (breast) milk to bulk up calories, and we'd cut a large hole in the bottle and kind of pour it down her because she could not afford to work too hard."

In reality, their ordeal had just begun. "After about a week at home, she didn't gain weight," says Stacey. The baby also appeared to be struggling to eat. "We had to bring her back to the hospital." During Abby's second hospitalization, Robbie says, "The doctors began to think there was something else wrong besides the heart defect. They started looking at various syndromes, but nothing was conclusive." Stacey was pumping milk constantly, and neither she nor Robbie was sleeping much. This time, Abby was hospitalized for three weeks, was given a feeding tube, and underwent many tests. In time, she moved from intensive care to a regular pediatric room. Nurses taught Stacey and Robbie how to manage her feeding tube, how to medicate Abby for the reflux from which she suffered, and how to monitor her oxygen-saturation levels. Finally, doctors said Abby could again return home; they still hoped to postpone her surgery for as long as possible.

Most people have an oxygen-saturation level near 100 percent, but Abby's levels were very low, from about 80 when she was doing well down to a very risky 60. When it fell to a dangerous level after two more weeks at home, Stacey and Robbie raced back to the hospital. Doctors told them to put their hazards on and drive fast, and that if they were pulled over, they should have the police call the hospital. During Abby's third hospital stay, she declined rapidly, and surgery was scheduled. "Their hands were forced," says Robbie. "They didn't want to do it, but she actually did quite well in the surgery. They were surprised." Surgeons successfully inserted a shunt into her artery.

"Nurses were about to let us in to see her after the surgery when she coded," says Stacey. To aid in resuscitating her, the medical team placed Abby on an ECMO (extracorporeal membrane oxygenation) machine, which does the work of the heart and lungs, so that Abby could stabilize and rest. Before she could be placed on an ECMO machine, however, a smaller surgical procedure was needed to insert a catheter into the artery in her neck. Again, Abby did well and bounced back.

During the next couple of weeks, "it was up and down," says Robbie. "One minute we were thinking she would survive this, and her heart is going to get stronger. But (surgeons) discovered when they opened her up that her heart muscle was very weak." Some doctors gave them reasons to hope, and others were not optimistic. "I don't think it was their fault. She did have really strong moments and really weak moments. But it was very frustrating," Robbie says. Stacey and Robbie were told they may have to make a choice to remove Abby from the ECMO machine, essentially removing her life support, if she did not improve, and that they should begin thinking about that decision. "You tell me how to do that," Stacey replied.

During their time in the hospital, Stacey and Robbie saw many other parents suffering. The ECMO unit was next to the burn unit, where adults and children were treated for horrible burns. Robbie says, "We saw parents whose child had died; they just wandered the halls not knowing what to do." Stacey says, "My faith is what caused me to be able to breathe." She said wise women had affected her throughout her life and had taught her that during crises, "You have choices to make. You're there in the suffering; it's not changing. Either I'm going to cry out to God for the grace to face this—even though it feels like hell on earth—or I'm going to totally lose control and not be good for myself or anyone else. I was making choices all the time." Robbie says he didn't know whether to pray for Abby to survive, possibly with a severe deformity, or let her die. "We had to live our faith and not worry about what our circumstances looked like," he says.

On June 8, at 5 a.m., Stacey and Robbie received a call that Abby had crashed again, and they needed to get the hospital. She had begun to bleed and doctors were trying to stop it. They were five minutes away. "We drove as fast as we could, (but when we arrived) she was already dead," Robbie says. She was 11 weeks old. Hospital staff dressed Abby in a beautiful smocked gown. "We held her and called our parents and spent some precious time with her—not enough," says Stacey. "It upset me that we couldn't just bring her home. I couldn't understand why the funeral home had to drive three hours to come get her. You know it's not rational, but you don't know how to think. It's so surreal. You think, this can't be *really* happening. You have moments where you think this has got to be a dream."

Stacey and Robbie were devastated—although later, they were at least a tiny bit grateful that they had not been asked to remove Abby from life support. They were also thankful that Abby's suffering had ended. "She was fighting very hard," Stacey says, and despite "amazing" care, she adds, "I do think she was suffering." Stacey had seen Abby's pain and discomfort when Abby came out of sedation. "That is so excruciating as a parent," she says, "to know you can't fix it."

Driving home from the hospital was very difficult. "(The hospital) had been our world for 11 weeks. You live in a vacuum," says Robbie, adding that they had only left to sleep and have an occasional dinner. "When you leave for the last time, it's sad driving away." They returned to Stacey's brother's house to pack their things and drove home "empty handed." As they saw others on the road, they were incredulous that these people were going about their lives "while we had to go home and pick out a casket," says Robbie. "I sat there and cried the entire time, and Stacey was strong"—although he adds that when Stacey had emotional breakdowns, he was the strong one.

Stacey says men and women mourn differently. "I needed to weep and wail, like the women in the Middle East." She feels that in the West, however, people's mourning is often cut short. Stacey felt surprising emotions, including "a feeling of hatred" against a pregnant woman at Target whom she didn't even know. And there were days when Stacey thought she was really losing it. "I called a friend one day and said, 'I'm going to the cemetery, and I'm going to dig her up.' I know that sounds pretty wacko or whatever to say that, but you're at such a point where you think, 'I'm not going to be able to live through this.'" Stacey says she appreciated that her friends listened without judgment, and told her the feelings were only natural. "That's what I needed," she says. Stacey also wanted to talk about her grief more than Robbie did, and this caused some conflict between them. He explained he couldn't make it through the workday if he placed all his focus on it. "We came to an agreement, and had wise people remind us that it's normal if we grieve differently," Stacey says.

Stacey and Robbie feel very fortunate that their marriage survived such a terrible blow. Although it's a widespread belief that the death of a child causes large numbers of marriages to fail, this is overstated. A 2006 study by Directions Research showed that only 16 percent of couples who experience the death of a child divorce— and less than half of those who split felt their child's death contributed to the divorce. Research suggests that the grieving process can actually bring a couple together. For Stacey and Robbie, that was the case. They did unite in their grief once they allowed one another to grieve in their own unique ways.

From Grief to Growing Family

After Abby's death, Robbie and Stacey were so fearful of going through something like that again that they didn't want to become pregnant. After a few weeks, however, they realized they were "letting fear rob us of the joy of more children," says Stacey. As soon as she was able, Stacey, who had been nursing, took medication to jump-start her cycle, and they quickly conceived. "I remember going in for the ultrasound and finding out it was a boy, not a girl. It stunned me; I began to cry. The emotion just shocked me. I felt guilty about my feelings." Stacey says she didn't struggle for long, though; in the spring of 1999, only 14 months after Abby's passing, Stacey and Robbie welcomed their second son, Steven, into the world.

Two years later, Stacey became pregnant yet again, but miscarried at nine weeks. "I felt the loss strongly," says Stacey, "but it wasn't as difficult as losing Abby. I felt it was merciful of God to allow that to happen rather than to carry, to deliver and to watch the suffering and then (see the child) die. It was still sad." Fortunately, Stacey, then only 30 years old, became pregnant just three months later. She asked two of her friends—an OBGYN and an ultrasound tech—to conduct an early ultrasound while Robbie was at work. When she learned she was carrying a girl, she said, "We had a big tear fest." Then she called Robbie, who was working with her sister and sister-in-law, and they all joined in the happy tears. Other than some early problems with reflux, daughter Betsy was born very healthy. "One of our happiest times was when Betsy was born," says Robbie. "It was almost like the culmination of our family." Stacey agrees, "We felt complete. After having lost a daughter and having two sons, the joy and sweetness of another girl was really special."

Robbie's Crisis and Recovery

And so it was with the history of the births of three children and the passing of two that Stacey faced the nightmare scenario of losing her husband on that hot August day in the ER. But Stacey found the strength to collect herself and focus on "what needed to be done, how to get Robbie out of there and getting the kids taken care of." As the ER staff searched for a trauma center for Robbie, a physician friend pulled some strings at the Regional Trauma Center of Memphis, which immediately sent a helicopter to pick Robbie up. "It was a miracle," Robbie says.

Once at the trauma center, doctors diagnosed Robbie with a gloving wound, in which the skin and muscles separate to form an open, bleeding pocket. It was, says Robbie, quite painful. He also suffered a broken vertebrae and hip. His leg was put in traction. The day after the accident, Robbie underwent a seven-hour hip-repair surgery. A wound vacuum was used to treat his back wound. Every few days, on four different occasions, the wound had to be reopened and cleaned due to infection concerns.

Robbie remained at the trauma center for 18 days. From the time he could open his eyes and talk, he asked if he would be able to walk and run again. His orthopedic surgeon was fairly confident he could walk and swim again, but was "very iffy" on running. Robbie was also eager to get back on the bike. The Olympics were on during his hospital stay, and he enthusiastically watched the triathlons.

After two and a half weeks, Robbie was sent home in a back brace. "I was fearful," says Robbie, who wasn't exactly eager to leave the comfort provided by the nurses at the hospital. This frustrated Stacey, who couldn't wait for Robbie to be home with the family; besides, the kids were not permitted to visit him in the ICU. The issue caused an argument, but realizing their differences on the matter were based on nerves and misunderstanding, they decided to cut each other some slack.

Stacey knew that caring for Robbie would be difficult, especially since they had decided to start home-schooling their children the year prior. As it turned out, their home-school situation was a great help, as they could coordinate school activities around Robbie's therapy needs and doctor's appointments. And because they had gotten an early start on the school year, putting the children ahead in their studies, the family could sleep in a bit when Robbie had rough nights—many nights, he was in such pain he couldn't sleep at all—without falling behind.

The family quickly fell into a routine. Robbie spent a lot of time lying in bed because he couldn't sit up past a 30-degree angle while wearing his back brace. Even in that position, he could contribute in some ways, such as assisting Betsy with phonics. It was difficult for Robbie, being unable to provide much help at home or to even pick up Betsy, but the children learned to pitch in. Nate, then 13, was strong enough to help Stacey lift Robbie or turn him to put his brace on. "The kids got the chance to help their dad and walk through this with him," Stacey says. In the long run, Robbie's accident helped unify the family and provided a great many teachable moments.

As if things weren't difficult enough, Robbie was laid off from his job while on short-term disability. As the newest member of his work team, he was the one who was cut when one position was eliminated. This substantially increased Robbie and Stacey's stress levels. Not only were they facing mounting hospital bills, they now faced the loss of Robbie's income and the possibility of being forced to relocate. But Robbie's manager, who felt horrible about the situation, worked tirelessly to find Robbie another position within the company—one that would enable the family to stay put. And friends and family members surprised and delighted the couple by taking up a collection for Robbie's medical expenses, most of which were paid as a result. "That really floored us," says Robbie. Stacey adds, "We've been left speechless many times."

By the end of September, doctors allowed Robbie to put weight on his leg; by the end of October, they told him he could begin walking. Still wearing his back brace, Robbie started with a walker, then moved to a cane. "I don't know if I'd call it 'walking' at that point. It was more like 'hobbling,'" says Stacey. He also began working with a physical therapist whose stated goal was to restore Robbie to his former athletic level. Although Robbie was often frustrated, he kept working, improving each week. One day in November, Stacey returned from running an errand to find Robbie riding his stationary bike. That December, he ran three miles by himself. "I never anticipated being able to run that far that soon," Robbie says. His wounds fully healed, and the neurologist gave him a full clearance.

Stacey says every single one of Robbie's physicians attributes his fast recovery to his stellar fitness level before the accident. Robbie had completed several triathlons and had run his first marathon at 30. "They were astonished at his recovery, considering his injuries. They typically see worse long-term effects," Stacey says, joking that Robbie can now sense atmospheric changes thanks to the metal screws and plate in his hip. "I was extremely fortunate and blessed with the outcome," Robbie says. He has returned to nearly 100 percent of his previous abilities.

For Robbie, the hardest thing was being taken care of. He found being unable to provide for his most basic needs humiliating. In their relationship, Robbie had always been the strong one; but during his convalescence, he had no strength in reserve. "I can't be strong for both of us," Robbie told Stacey, adding "I can just barely be strong enough for me right now." For Stacey, that was difficult; Robbie had always looked on the bright side. Even so, he says, "Stacey was such a great nurse," noting that some wives could never have done what Stacey did. For Robbie, Stacey was "a rock." He cites one incident in which, about a week after returning home, he fell ill with a virus and vomited all night. Normally, Robbie handled the children's throw-up messes because Stacey could hardly stand it, but this time she held the bucket for Robbie all night because he couldn't sit up. "It was just a miserable night, and I couldn't go the bathroom. She took care of me," Robbie says. "These are telling moments. When you say for better or worse, you don't really think of what you'll have to face." He adds, "I've told my son when you're looking for a wife, you need someone you are spiritually compatible with, because when those tough times come, your relationship will be tested, and you need someone to build you up."

Finding their Happy Place

Robbie and Stacey had been through so much since they met on a softball field during the summer of 1987, when he was 17 and she was 15. Both say they had high standards that were reinforced by their parents, which included that anyone they date would be someone they would consider marrying. Dating unwisely creates a lot of disappointment, Stacey says, because it's easy to fall in love with the wrong person. Still, Stacey was a little "freaked out" that she might marry the only guy she had dated seriously. She broke up with Robbie during her senior year to check out her other options, but ultimately came back to him "because I knew I wasn't going to find anyone better than Robbie."

In 1990, after attending Arkansas State University, they became engaged following a performance of *Les Miserables* and married a year later. Because of their small budget, they gratefully accepted a trip to Disney World, which Robbie's parents had won, as their honeymoon. Just before Robbie's accident, Robbie and Stacey returned to Disney World for the first time since their honeymoon, this time with their three children. "To be there again with a thirteen-, eight- and six-year old was really neat," Stacey says. Robbie calls it one of the best times during their marriage because they relived their newlywed memories while also seeing their children's joy in being there.

Despite their great love for their children, Robbie and Stacey say their marriage takes a higher priority in their home—and the children know that. "You're not going to be with your children forever. We have plans for when our kids are gone, but while they are here, our lives are centered around their care," Stacey says. She adds that she and Robbie like to watch cycling and hope to follow the Tour de France through Europe one year. "It's more the day-to-day companionship that keeps us going," says Stacey. "Yeah, the passion, too, but it's the sharing." They recently celebrated an anniversary at a solitary mountain lodge. "We watched movies and the falling snow," says Stacey. "Those things make our day that much more special. We just want to be together."

At their pastor's urging, the Johnsons—particularly Stacey—have shared their experiences to help other couples who have lost children overcome grief. For Stacey, reaching back, taking the hand of someone who has just started down that road, and figuratively walking a few miles together is a beautiful thing. She tells them, "You're going to survive, and I know you can't believe it, but you are even going to be happy again. You really will." Then, she just makes herself available for when they are ready to talk. "They just want to know you've been there," she says.

Robbie says the painful experiences in their lives have taught them "lessons that are immeasurable." Stacey agrees, adding that one lesson she learned was to show more grace toward other people, wherever you are. She also recognizes that she is not in control of her circumstances. Neither Robbie nor Stacey would remove the pain they lived through if it meant removing what they had gained in the process. Stacey says she would love to have Abby back and wishes Robbie had never been hit, but these crises gave them an opportunity to live by their faith, and it gave them strength. "I've grown in so many ways," she says. "People who have not gone through real pain like that, it's not that their faith is not real, but it's amazing how much more solid it becomes when it's been tested," Robbie says. But now that they've found a happier stage of life, Stacey says with a smile, "We are not so pious to say, 'bring it on' (more pain). We'd like to pretty much coast from here on out."

Robbie wasn't afraid of going back on the road on his bike, but Stacey had to work through her fears. She knew she could whine and manipulate him into not riding anymore if it meant that much to her, but says, "I felt strongly that I should not ask him to give up something he was so passionate about." She chose again to not live in fear. She also knew Robbie was not one to take risks. One day, when it was raining, she asked him not to go, and he stayed home. "She didn't have to twist my arm; I don't like to ride in the rain," Robbie says.

Robbie and Stacey make choices each day—to embrace life, to prioritize their marriage, to appreciate their children, to love one another, and to overcome their fears. When Robbie rises early and sets off for another long-distance bike ride, it's almost as if he has been taken apart and put back together again—this time with a greater appreciation for life and the love in his life.

Lesson:

Forgiveness is a gift for the giver and the receiver.

CHAPTER 3:

PREVAILING AFTER AN AFFAIR

Considering that approximately 65 percent of couples divorce after infidelity, Ron and Nancy Anderson are an exception. When you add the fact that they have raised an autistic son, endured a financial crisis, and the loss of an infant son, however, the success of their marriage is truly remarkable. Their early marriage was a battle, but what they have today is pure joy.

A Rocky Beginning

Ron and Nancy Anderson had no idea of the challenges they would encounter when they married on a beautiful June day in 1978 in La Mirada, California. They made each other laugh. They had fun. They were madly in love. Wasn't that all that mattered?

Ron had been in the Army and had traveled the world before returning to California to settle down. He was working as an accountant and a stand-up comic and also attending school at Cerritos Junior College when he noticed a pretty girl on a park bench on campus reading a book about Groucho Marx. The book cover caught his attention because of his interest in comedy. He was instantly attracted and asked her how the book was. The girl, Nancy, a fellow student, was cool to Ron's advances. Since moving to California from Minnesota, she preferred blond, tan surfers—a species she had just discovered, to her delight.

In the coming weeks, Ron saw Nancy on campus and frequently asked her out for coffee, lunch, or dinner. He asked her out at least 10 times before she finally agreed. As a financially struggling student who rarely had a dollar in her pocket, the offers of food finally worked. Eventually they went out to dinner and both had a "wonderful time."

During their courtship, Ron and Nancy worked very hard to please each other. She enjoyed his sense of humor; they laughed a lot, and enjoyed being together. As an extrovert, Ron had many friends; he never met a stranger. According to Nancy, Ron was so friendly that he had even invited a homeless man to have lunch with him. Nancy was impressed with his social skills and charm, although she was clearly an introvert.

They knew they had fun together, and they thought being married would be as easy as hanging out had been. They didn't notice their differences, including very different family backgrounds, until after they were married. They admit they didn't understand how a marriage should work.

"After we got married, we got lazy about looking out for each other's needs," says Nancy. Ron still had lots of friends he hung out with, while Nancy preferred to stay home. He didn't "shift gears" into married life. He was more like a single guy with a wife, says Nancy—although he didn't cheat on her. Nancy says she felt like Ron's pet, whom he had trapped into marriage.

Ron and Nancy both lived independent lives. She didn't know about his finances and friends. They didn't share feelings or concerns. Each made decisions about purchases and activities without consulting the other—for example, Nancy bought a new TV without consulting Ron—which led to many arguments.

Soon, they were fighting non-stop. They argued about money, house decorations—anything that came up. It was nothing like the *Leave it to Beaver* family that Nancy grew up in and expected to "just happen" in her life. The life her parents created was an impossible ideal that Nancy, a mere 22 years old, didn't feel she could attain.

Nancy was starting to feel especially isolated. Her family lived far away, and she had few friends nearby. Ron's family lived in the area, but Nancy didn't connect with them. Nancy says Ron's parents frequently screamed obscenities at one another. "Theirs was a very chaotic home, and I wasn't attracted to chaos," she says. Ron had grown up watching his alcoholic father hit and cheat on his mother and belittle his sisters. While Ron was never physically abusive or unfaithful to Nancy, he mimicked some of the angry words and actions he grew up with. His parents were married in 1949 and, while they remain married, "they still hate each other." Having those role models did not teach Ron to be a good husband.

"I was a selfish jerk," he concludes easily. Married at 26, Ron lacked almost every skill needed for a strong marriage, he says. "I didn't understand that marriage was about more than just me." Nancy and Ron say the biggest skills they lacked were communication skills and empathy. They were both unable to see the other person's point of view. There was no teamwork. Nancy describes their early marriage as playing singles tennis on opposing sides. "We were each other's biggest enemy," says Nancy. In a good marriage, she says, you should be playing doubles tennis—on the same side—fighting against adversity together.

After a while, they moved to a new county and had few friends nearby. They didn't relate to their neighbors and hadn't yet sought out a church to attend. They didn't have solid marriages around them from which to model. The isolation made them feel yet farther apart from each other. They expressed their anxiety and unhappiness by fighting. "It was almost as if we had one continuous argument that just stopped when one of us left the house and started right up again when we were both home," explained Nancy, who longed for what was missing in her marriage.

Specifically, Nancy longed for what she saw in her parents' marriage—companionship, love, teamwork, a peaceful coexistence. Married more than 60 years, Nancy's parents worked together and laughed together. They had very little conflict. They still really like each other and depend on each other. They've helped one another through major illnesses. When Nancy looked at her own marriage in comparison, she says, "I knew we didn't have (those qualities), but we didn't know how to get there."

Rebuilding After Infidelity

Nancy and Ron didn't have much love in their marriage. When Nancy did fall in love again, it was not with her husband. Instead, a relationship with a married co-worker, Jake, had started slowly brewing. They had frequent team-building meetings together and lunches away from the office. They began to confide in one another the discontent they felt in their marriages. One day, during a meeting, Jake pressed his knee against Nancy's; she didn't pull away. That was the spark—the moment it all began. This is also where her major regrets start.

Nancy and Ron had only been married a few years—they were relative newlyweds—but she began dreaming about Jake's kiss and the scent of his cologne. Jake began to fill the void left in her marriage. Jake told Nancy she was smart, funny, and beautiful, and encouraged her in every way. Their secret, passionate trysts provided excitement and masked her sadness. Soon, Nancy and Jake were pledging their love and planning to leave their spouses to be together. Nancy's marriage was all but over.

Except that it wasn't. In fact, Ron and Nancy would not have believed then that they would rebuild their marriage and develop a level of intimacy, trust, and caring they only dreamed of. They have now celebrated more than 30 years of marriage, and have overcome many other significant obstacles.

Ready to Leave

When Nancy told a friend at work she was leaving her husband, the friend cheered her on. "Good for you. I'm so proud of you. Life's too short for you to be unhappy," she was told. Nancy calls that the "big lie" that she believed—the lie that life is about seeking happiness for oneself. Nancy explains that she had been primarily seeking self-fulfillment. If Ron could be happy at the same time that she found happiness, that would be a nice byproduct, but it wasn't essential. At its core, the statement, "I deserve to be happy" is a selfish statement about putting one's needs above others, she says, adding that "no marriage based on selfishness will work."

By this point in the affair, Jake had left his wife and was now waiting in the wings. The spark Nancy felt for him had turned to electricity. Their romantic future plans now included moving to a cabin in the woods together.

Nancy wasn't ready to be honest with her husband about Jake, so she told Ron she needed some space and time to herself to work things out. Ron begged her not to leave, but she told him she needed some time alone. Ron acquiesced, believing that giving her the time would help to eventually heal their marriage. Soon, Nancy had rented a hotel room, then an apartment, and started planning a new life. Ron was confused, devastated, and consumed with grief.

Not long after, Ron called Nancy and asked her to come home. Neither his tears nor the sadness in his voice persuaded her to change course. Even after a friend called Nancy to tell her Ron was completely broken, Nancy told her friend that she loved her new freedom and wasn't going back to him.

Fortunately, Nancy's parents, whom Nancy had shielded from her troubles, derailed the chain of events that might otherwise have come to pass. Though they lived some distance away, they sensed that something was very wrong in Nancy's life. One evening, their intuition prompted them to call Ron and Nancy's home to speak to Nancy; coincidentally, although Nancy had moved out, she happened to be home when her parents called, picking up some things while Ron was at a work conference.

Nancy's mom told Nancy she was having trouble sleeping, sure that something was terribly wrong in Nancy's life. Nancy denied that there were any problems. Unable to get through, Nancy's mom passed the phone to Nancy's dad, who told her that her mother was usually right about these things and she needed to come clean if there was something wrong.

They persisted through her lies of everything being fine until she finally told them her marriage was on the rocks. She told them she didn't think it was going to work and that she planned to leave her husband. Her parents first made sure Nancy was not being abused. Then they reminded her of her marriage vows and asked her what she had been doing to save the marriage. She said she hadn't gone to counseling or asked anyone to help them, but she just wasn't happy and Ron didn't treat her well. Nancy's parents finally convinced Nancy that her marriage vows trumped her own happiness and asked her to at least wait there for Ron to come home from his conference and talk to him.

A Turning Point

What followed that night was a very unlikely about-face, during which Nancy finally stopped running from her mistakes and sat face-to-face with the fact that she was having an affair outside of her marriage. Nothing justified what she was doing to Ron, and she knew it. She had been hiding from what she knew to be true. She says she realized that she was a fraud. "I had high standards for others, but I didn't live up to them. I was a Christian but didn't act like it. I was a good girl, but I wasn't. Everything was upside down and fake." It was then that Nancy's upbringing in the church started to pour out, and she began to talk to God.

Nancy spent several hours waiting for Ron on the couch, entrenched in a personal battle. She thought about her life, her marriage, and her feelings for Jake, finally coming to understand how wrong she had been. Only then did she start to see that she was an equal contributor to her bad marriage. She started to understand that what she and Jake had wasn't real love. It was exciting, but built on lies.

Any man who would cheat on his wife and leave his two children to be with her would probably not make an ideal mate, she concluded. And clearly she wasn't winning any awards as a wife either. What made her think things would be perfect with another man?

After much anguish and thought, she confessed, prayed for forgiveness, and asked God to save her marriage. But she didn't know if Ron could ever forgive her.

Ron returned early from the conference, still distraught about his marriage. He was shocked to return home and find his wife there, and even more so when she said she wanted to work things out. They sat down to talk, and to his surprise, she confessed that she had been having an affair. They both agreed if they were going to try to salvage the marriage, she needed quit her job the next day, and never see Jake again.

The next day she called her boss and explained the situation. He accepted her resignation, wished her well, and supported her desire to save her marriage. Then Ron and Nancy both spoke to Jake on the phone and asked him to never contact Nancy again. It was a difficult, but necessary step, Nancy says. Jake reluctantly agreed, and they never spoke again.

At this point, all Ron and Nancy had was a commitment to stay together. They still lacked the insight to move forward successfully, given their tumultuous past. They didn't know how to talk to each other without yelling and blaming. Nancy says she used to take almost any comment from Ron as a personal insult and was very defensive.

Nancy's parents invited them for a visit to help guide them through reconciliation. They helped her to truly confess her wrongdoing to Ron and ask him for forgiveness, and then gave Ron the time to decide if he could honestly do so without using it against her in the future. The next morning, Ron decided he would indeed forgive her and they would move forward with whatever they needed to do to repair the damage.

Each time Ron recounts the story, he gets tears in his eyes, explaining, "The minute she asked for my forgiveness, God passed the pain and sorrow out of my heart." He says it was like being miraculously healed of cancer. To this day, he has not held ill will toward her about the affair. Many men have asked him how this is possible, to be so free of anger and jealousy. He says they avoided talking about the details of the affair, and he saw the pain, guilt, and regret in his wife. That was enough.

Besides, Ron says, he had enough guilt for his own actions. There were three things he had been doing that frequently hurt his wife. First, when they got into big arguments, he would call Nancy "vulgar obscenities." He shudders to think of it now. Second, he frequently tried to talk her out of her feelings. For example, if she said, "I don't feel like I have any friends," Ron would remind her of her last lunch meeting with a friend and tell her she shouldn't feel that way. He didn't see that his wife just needed a listening ear, a hug and reassurance. Finally, he says Nancy was frequently the brunt of his public and private jokes. In his childhood home, everyone was teased, and a quick wit was admired. But this made Nancy feel humiliated. It took Ron about three years to get out of the habit of doing this after he made a decision to stop. Instead of telling Nancy not to be so sensitive, he learned to say, "I'm sorry. I'll do better next time." Nancy could tell Ron was making an effort, and she began to let it go.

The weeks and months after the reconciliation were not magical, happy days, but both Ron and Nancy forged a new commitment to making their marriage a success. And slowly, one day at a time, they worked on their own behavior. Once the foundation was repaired, they rebuilt their marriage, brick by brick. They attended marriage counseling for about six months. They're not sure how good the counselor was, since he only asked them questions, but add that they did come up with a lot of answers on their own, so perhaps he led them in the right direction.

Even though their reconciliation was hard work, the difference, explain Ron and Nancy, was that before, they were on the wrong path going in opposite directions. But after the reconciliation, they were moving together, up a really steep mountain. "We were committed to doing it even though it was hard, because there were little glimpses of hope," says Nancy.

Nancy says she realized that love is more than a feeling; it is a decision. When she decided to act in a loving way toward her husband, her feelings soon followed. They tried to be encouraging and corrected one another's errors as they learned how to share, how to trust, and how to love again. "It took us years just to learn how not to be jerks," they joke. They attended marriage retreats, starting dating each other again, and learned to change bad behaviors.

They learned to behave more lovingly by using positive reinforcement. Instead of focusing on each mistake as before, they pointed out when the other did something right. They were more patient with one another and showed more mercy. "I saw that he was sincerely trying to change, and that made the difference," says Nancy. "He really did feel bad when he made a mistake. I felt like I owed it to him (to be patient) after we got back together. The scales were tipped in his favor." Although it defied logic, she says, the more she could see Ron's point of view and help make him happy, the more he responded back in a positive way. As a small example, when she asked herself what Ron would like for dinner, she found him to be very grateful and loving in return.

When they saw small successes, they believed that bigger successes were possible. The process of building their marriage took about five years. Near the end of that process, Nancy and Ron saw a different marriage counselor, whom they said helped them adapt to different life issues and learn more about their marriage. "He had a lot of profound statements," Nancy says.

Ron says he read many books about how to understand women and made it his goal to really learn about Nancy as a person. Similarly, Nancy tried to understand the male perspective and the importance of certain things, such as sex and clean laundry, to her husband. Over the years, they have come to understand how beautifully complementary masculinity and femininity are in a marriage when they are working together. For example, Ron was unfamiliar with tenderness and vulnerability. In his childhood home, he had learned to "protect his underbelly" rather than be vulnerable. He can now trust and be vulnerable and appreciate the tenderness that Nancy brings to the relationship. Nancy appreciates the strength and power that Ron's masculinity brings. In their early relationship, Nancy says she treated Ron like a little boy and corrected him as a mother would. She didn't consult his opinion or say she trusted his judgment when making decisions. Now she can say, "You're a smart guy; you can make that decision." They say these feminine and masculine qualities are true for all marriages. "That's the beauty of marriage and how we were created to be. We are more powerful together than either of us is alone," says Nancy.

They developed protective rules to guard their marriage against temptation, and Nancy wrote a book about those guidelines entitled *Avoiding the Greener Grass Syndrome*. At the time of her affair, she was looking at the greener grass of another relationship, not realizing she was the one who needed to change. They don't place themselves in vulnerable situations, such as having dinner alone with a member of the opposite sex.

As a result of their marriage turnaround, many years ago their church leaders asked them to teach a marriage class. They were horrified at first to talk publicly of their trials, but agreed to do it. Decades later, they are involved in marriage retreats and seminars and find they are good at helping strengthen other marriages. They also mentor young couples at their church. They developed teamwork by working with each of their strengths. Nancy likes the seminar preparation and technical parts. Ron likes to tell stories and make it funny.

They say they have learned so much from helping other couples. They study and read about marriage and learn from others as they impart their own experience. They provide some emergency marriage counseling to couples who seek them out, but they only counsel others as a couple. When a woman wanted only Ron to counsel her about her marriage, they responded that they were a package deal. It's not that they don't trust one another, but they feel it's a way to insulate and protect their marriage.

They are so thankful to have avoided divorce, which they have seen cause "immeasurable suffering" in many around them, including devastating children and leading to financial disaster. Their success has led them to become involved in other organizations that support marriage. "People say they don't need a piece of paper that shows they are married. If I hadn't had that piece of paper, I would never have gone back," says Nancy. "That piece of paper meant and still means a great deal to me."

Ron says one of the biggest mistakes they made early in their marriage was becoming isolated and not being accountable to anyone. He adds that every couple is naïve when they are getting married. "You see the fireworks and chemistry, but there is an earthquake coming that you don't see. You have to find your way through it—it's a journey."

Now they surround themselves with like-minded couples who love them enough to point out when they are acting poorly, such as speaking disrespectfully to their spouse. They go out weekly with a peer couple with whom they talk and share troubles and give and receive counsel. They also see Nancy's parents each week, as they have relocated to California. "They are spiritual giants to us," says Nancy.

Their Journey Continues

Life has certainly been a journey for Ron and Nancy. The skills they gained after rebuilding their marriage were vital to getting through later challenges together.

Not long after their marriage was back on track, they decided to have a child. Their son, Nick, who was born in 1985, is still the joy of their lives. Now grown—really grown at 6 feet 5 inches and 225 pounds—he was diagnosed with autism as a young child. Nancy spent his childhood researching treatments and taking him to various therapies. Thankfully, he is functioning well and has progressed to a fairly independent life. He lives with his parents, but has a job and volunteers as a theater usher.

His diagnosis and care did cause some conflict in the marriage. Ron was in denial about Nick's autism for some time, and he thought Nancy was "too soft" on Nick. Nancy, who spent all her time with Nick and knew his limitations, felt Ron was "too hard" on him. Over time, as Ron saw visibly disabled children who could do more than Nick could do and came to realize Nancy was right, he realized he needed to adjust his thinking. This transition period was difficult, but by then Ron and Nancy had built a strong marriage that could withstand disagreements. Nancy was gentler in her communication —for instance, leaving a brief article about the signs of autism for Ron to read and come to his own conclusion. They supported one another and had many friends who included Nick in activities and treated him with kindness.

The birth of their son further solidified their family commitment. "When Nick was born, I decided I wasn't going anywhere. I would fight to the death to keep our family together. We loved him so much and could see we were both very necessary to him," says Nancy. "I didn't even mentally consider other men as attractive after that." Ron also became more committed after becoming a parent.

Yet another blow came when Nick was five and Nancy became pregnant again. An amniocentesis showed that their baby had Trisomy 18, an abnormality which makes life outside the womb nearly unsustainable. The doctor, as well as some friends and family members, encouraged them to end the pregnancy. However, Ron and Nancy were in agreement that they would carry the pregnancy to term. Nancy says she now understands that those who advised her to end the pregnancy were only trying to spare her pain. But at the time, it felt wrong. "I couldn't abandon my baby any more than I could abandon Nick," she says. Ron didn't want to talk about it, although he also didn't want to end the pregnancy.

Once the news was out, friends and family pulled away, not knowing what to say or do. Even Ron didn't want to rub Nancy's belly and sing songs the way he did when she was pregnant with Nick. For Nancy, with a baby moving inside of her, the experience was very real and full of sadness and loneliness. At the same time, Nick had a lot of needs, and Nancy was busy caring for him, just making it through each day for several months. Their son, Timmy, lived only 13 minutes after birth. They held him and sang to him and provided all the love they could in a tragically short time.

Neither Ron nor Nancy properly grieved Timmy's death at the time. Ron admits he probably hasn't ever really dealt with it, but merely stored it away in a "little box deep inside." Nancy chose to move on and keep busy. It wasn't until two years later, experiencing deep depression and anxiety, that she made time to grieve with a counselor. By this time, Nick was more stable, and she finally felt it was safe to fall apart.

While they regret not being able to have more children, Ron and Nancy love having fun with Nick and taking him on many trips—from cruises to a trip to Israel.

Ron says with each new obstacle they faced, they were able to flex the muscles of their now-strong marriage. Every test seemed to bring them closer together. "You have to be strong for the next crisis," he says.

That was certainly the case when the real-estate market in California took a nosedive, carrying much of their financial investments with it. Ron was "playing Monopoly" with their money, slowly building up their real-estate assets, usually on borrowed money, then "flipping" the houses. They didn't see any potential down side until it was too late. They lost one house during the turmoil and lost a lot of rental income as rental prices also dropped.

There was no finger-pointing when their financial crisis hit. They simply tightened their belts, spending the next five years digging themselves completely out of debt. They purchased what they needed using cash only, and Nancy took a part-time job to help pay the debt down. They didn't even argue. "We put everything on the table and worked it out," they explained.

What they have managed to work out in more than 30 years of marriage is remarkable. "We are absolutely amazed at what we almost lost," says Nancy. "It's not that we toughed it out, we really like each other. I'd still choose him." She adds that she has all those things she longed for—companionship, love, teamwork, a peaceful coexistence—and it's even better than she had hoped.

Finally, they feel they are both playing on the same side of the net, fighting against common enemies. "It's better than we could have ever imagined," says Nancy. "When we do couples events or retreats, he gets tears in his eyes talking about how much he adores and loves me. I had no idea it could be like that." With Nancy now in her mid 50s, Ron still sees her as the pretty young girl on the park bench. "He sees the best of me. He really is a different person. He already had a great personality, but the tenderness rounded him out. We have a lot of moments now where he grabs my hand and says, 'I adore you.'"

Ron adds, "I have an incredible life with an incredible wife, and I missed out on a few years of it. I just wish I'd known some of this stuff sooner!"

The Andersons provide a remarkable example of how tragedies can strike a marriage, even one after another. They seem to have become stronger with each one, as they come closer together and rely on one another's strengths to weather each storm. Thankfully, for the time being, the storm has passed, replaced by blue skies and sunshine.

Lesson:

Love is not enough to make a marriage work;
it takes commitment and hard work.

CHAPTER 4:

IS LOVE ENOUGH?

When couples face a marital crisis, they tend to be in one of two camps. In the first camp, some decision or action by one of the partners, such as alcohol abuse or an affair, puts the marriage at risk. In the other very large camp, life hits hard—without preparation or warning. The crisis can spring from an illness, a disaster, a family death, or other event. It can strip a marriage down to almost nothing. It can peel away at every level of your person, until you aren't sure what is left of you. The worst crises test your relationships and maybe even your will to live. Sometimes—if you're tenacious enough—you can make it through; but often, another battle awaits.

From Traditional to Terrified

In 1982, LaRita Jacobs was a happy 20-year-old newlywed attending college with Kurt, her husband of seven months. The couple had their lives on track and planned out. But on what started as one average Saturday night, their lives were violently derailed.

High-school sweethearts, Kurt and LaRita had been together for three years before marrying. They shared traditional, conservative values and wanted to save sex for marriage. After earning associate's degrees, they decided to wed and to live together while they finished college. It wasn't an easy decision. Some family members thought they were too young to marry and that one or both of them might not finish their degrees. Moreover, both had a lot to lose financially by marrying instead of living together. Once married, LaRita lost the Social Security and VA benefits she had received since her father's death in a work-related accident. Likewise, Kurt lost access to his father's disability benefits, which were contingent on him being a full-time student and a dependent. These checks, totaling about $700 a month, had helped them through their time at a local community college in Virginia during a period when rent was only $175 a month, including utilities. Still, they were decisive, and the marriage won out. To pay for schooling, they both took out student loans and worked side jobs.

LaRita and Kurt decided to move 14 hours away from home to attend their third year of college at Western Kentucky University, which had a strong liberal arts program for LaRita, as well as a well-regarded electrical engineering program for Kurt. They found a small apartment and registered as full-time students. They reveled in their time together and were starting to enjoy their sex life, although LaRita admits they were still "getting over all that good Christian guilt." Their social lives were a bit of a challenge, however, due to the dearth of other married couples on campus. "We were figuring out how to be married and how to socialize with a bunch of people who couldn't even imagine being married," she says.

To make ends meet, LaRita applied for a babysitting job with a service that fielded calls from clients who needed child care and dispatched approved caregivers to their homes. The setup worked fine for LaRita, with the service taking a portion of the income in exchange for setting up all the appointments. One evening, LaRita was dispatched to the home of a couple in town to watch their two young children. When she arrived, the client informed LaRita that his wife was running an errand and would be back shortly. He showed her the two sleeping children upstairs in their bedrooms, and gave her a quick tour of the house, including where the baby's bottles were kept. Afterward, LaRita excused herself to use the bathroom. When she came back out, the client viciously attacked her from behind, tying her hands and holding a knife to her throat. LaRita screamed for help and fought as hard as she could, but she was no match for the stronger man. Moreover, LaRita quickly discovered that he had placed weapons throughout the room, tucking ropes and knives under the edge of the couch and laying out other objects with which he could hit her. "They were all at hand. It was well staged," she says.

LaRita was raped and severely injured, struck repeatedly in the head with a tent stake. LaRita was certain she was going to die, but was in such shock that she "wasn't real concerned about being killed." In excruciating pain, she even began to lose the will to live. But then she envisioned her mother's and husband's faces. She imagined the horror they would endure if they were told LaRita had been found "dead and naked in a ditch somewhere." She says, "I couldn't live with that. I couldn't do that." She regained her desire to survive and began searching for a way out.

"I was screaming, and he would tell me to shut up. When I shut up, he quit hitting me. I realized the intent wasn't to beat the hell out of me, it was to get me to shut up." So instead of screaming, LaRita started questioning her attacker. "Who are you?" she asked him repeatedly. "What are you doing? Why are you doing this?" He told her not to try that psychological stuff, but she didn't relent. She asked about his kids, his wife, anything she could think of. She continued talking until suddenly, "things went from horrifying to absolutely bizarre." LaRita believes that her attacker was high on drugs, and that as she was talking to him, he started coming down from his high. He abruptly stopped the attack "and looked at me like he's never seen me before." He appeared panicked as he surveyed the woman in front of him—propped against the wall, hands tied, covered in blood, and naked from the waist down—and asked, "What the f--k have I done?"

The man started yelling. "They're gonna kill me!" he said, over and over. (LaRita thought he was referring to the police, but she later learned that the man's brother had been killed in jail after a rape conviction. The fact that LaRita's assailant had requested a babysitter over the age of 18 meant he likely knew the punishment for raping a juvenile would be more severe than for an adult.) He wanted to take her away in the car, but LaRita, knowing she had to take control, said no. She knew that being moved to a second location would almost certainly mean her death. She insisted he call his wife, who, she had learned, was at work. Surprisingly, the man agreed, but he refused to speak into the phone. Instead, he held it up to LaRita's mouth—her hands were still tied. She said, "My name is LaRita Jacobs. I'm a babysitter at your house. There's been an emergency, and you need to come home right away." The wife replied that she didn't have a babysitter; her husband was watching the children. LaRita just repeated the same sentence several times. The woman hung up and called back, just to verify that LaRita was, indeed, at the house; finally convinced, she agreed to come.

Before the man's wife came home, he untied LaRita, and she got dressed. "There was blood everywhere, and the place was a wreck." Eventually, the wife, escorted by a young male co-worker who had given her a ride, walked in the door. Upon seeing the scene, the woman pushed her co-worker back outside. "What is going on here?" the co-worker said; the wife replied, "We'll take care of it." LaRita realized then that this woman's focus was protecting her husband; she knew she had to stay in control.

Thanks to her profuse bleeding and obvious injuries, LaRita was able to convince the woman to call Kurt to tell him that there had been an emergency and he needed to come over. On his way out, Kurt grabbed a pocketknife. He knew something was wrong, but he had no idea of the extent until he got there. LaRita, anxious about how her husband would feel seeing her disheveled and hurt, went into the bathroom and tried to clean up. "I knew I looked horrible, but I didn't want to stress him out." She washed a little and tried to ignore the red blood streaking through her long, blond hair as she re-pinned one of her braids that had fallen down.

Kurt arrived, but LaRita, still focused on getting to safety, wouldn't tell him what had happened. Quickly, however, Kurt realized that LaRita had been attacked. When he began yelling at her assailant, both LaRita and her attacker's wife begged him to calm down. Recognizing that the man and wife were unstable, and that LaRita needed medical treatment, Kurt grabbed the phone and dialed 911. "My wife has been assaulted," he told the operator. "We need an ambulance." He kept the couple at bay until help arrived. "I was trying to take care of my wife, because I could see she was hurt," he says. "I felt I could keep things in order and keep [LaRita's assailant] there until police arrived."

In a short time, police, an ambulance, and a rescue squad arrived at the home. As EMTs treated LaRita's injuries on the scene, she took in the flashing lights and the blood splatters—and a three-year-old girl "walking across the room, eyes big as saucers and tears running down her cheeks." LaRita's assailant's "flaky wife" had brought her daughter downstairs to say goodbye to her dad, who was being taken away by police. LaRita told the EMT, "Somebody needs to get that little girl out of here."

Fortunately, LaRita's injuries were not life-threatening. After being treated and receiving 28 stitches in her head, LaRita and Kurt returned to their apartment. Her attacker was arrested and she pressed charges. There was no question of guilt; the police had been called to the scene and had collected loads of evidence. But Kurt and LaRita were devastated. "We were blown away; we couldn't do anything," LaRita said. Kurt says those initial days felt like a blur. "I was on automatic, doing what I had to do." Craving the comfort of their families, they decided to drop out of school and move back home.

LaRita's parents and brother drove to Kentucky, rented a U-Haul, and packed up the apartment while Kurt and LaRita met with school officials to withdraw from their classes. Explaining why she felt she needed to leave, LaRita showed her stitches to the college administrators, who helpfully credited back their out-of-state tuition despite it being past the deadline. Upon their return to Virginia, LaRita and Kurt moved into Kurt's parent's house, where there was more space. Soon thereafter, Kurt and LaRita experienced financial problems; fortunately, Kurt's parents were willing and able to help out.

As grateful as they were for their families' help, the simple fact was that, in the space of just a few days, Kurt and LaRita had gone from being a happy, independent couple to living in a spare bedroom, with all their belongings packed in the garage. It was very hard, says LaRita. "It felt like your parents came over and said, 'You can't play house anymore.'" Kurt felt every imaginable emotion, including anger and shock. Then, he says, "I remember being numb. I didn't remember feeling anything else."

Healing after Stranger Rape

In her work with other victims, LaRita has seen many marriages in which the wife is raped that don't survive. She's not surprised, because of the effect on her own marriage. In her and Kurt's experience, their relationship changed quickly and dramatically, evolving into something completely different. Instead of being the leader she had always been, LaRita suddenly became very passive. For more than six months, she lost all desire to be held, hugged, or touched in a sexual manner, preferring to be loved and cuddled as a child would be. She needed her husband to act in a comforting parent role rather than as a spouse. Thankfully, however, she progressed through her recovery, which involved steps very similar to those involved in overcoming grief, like anger and denial. LaRita began seeing rape counselors, who were trained volunteers; sometimes Kurt went along. Kurt and LaRita also attended marriage counseling to help get back on track. "We had to rediscover all the other ways in which we could go on with our lives," she says. The recovery—which was traumatic and changed LaRita profoundly—seemed very long to her. "It took a long time before I felt the basic me was still me," she says, although she still felt a loss of innocence. For Kurt, it seemed shorter—it was between six months to a year before he felt they were "back to normal."

Kurt took a few months off work until, as he says, he "got back a little of his sanity." Then he began looking for a job and taking classes part-time. "It took a while for him to be able to feel like he could leave me alone," LaRita explains. Both LaRita and Kurt acknowledge that they were fortunate to be able to fall back on their parents to care for them, noting that it would have been much harder to go on with life, pretending that things were normal, had that not been the case. LaRita took a little more time off than Kurt, and then resumed her schooling at a community college. Motivating her were the memories of those who had told her she was too young to marry and that she'd never finish school. "I had to finish college to prove I could," she says. Kurt and LaRita took turns, one taking classes full-time and working part-time while the other took classes part-time and worked full-time, until both of their degrees were completed.

LaRita stayed in touch with a victim's assistance representative in Kentucky, who told her the case was eventually plea bargained instead of going to trial. Her assailant received a 25-year sentence, but despite having a previous assault conviction was expected to be released within five years due to jail overcrowding. LaRita was angry that he would likely be out on the street before his 40th birthday, and able to hurt someone else. She even hoped he would die in jail like his brother, so that no other woman would have to suffer as she did. Going through what she did would have been worth a lot more, said LaRita, if "a lot of others would be protected." She continues, "Knowing that I didn't have that power was very frustrating. I knew that at some point it was likely he would be released to be a danger again." But after many discussions, she and Kurt opted to not be informed when he was released for parole or to attend his parole hearing. In the end, LaRita says, she and Kurt decided, "What purpose did it serve for us to know (if and when he was released)? I couldn't have done anything about it." They didn't want to continue to look back. So, they looked forward. They decided to move on with their lives. Eventually, life became stable. They bought a little house. They forged a new plan.

A New Battle: Chronic Illness and Depression

After LaRita was attacked, she and Kurt made a conscious decision to hold off on having children until they could sort through their lives and make a new plan. Four years later, they were ready; in 1986, they gave birth to a daughter, Laura. Although she was born prematurely, she grew healthy and strong. LaRita worked part-time after the birth, then obtained her master's degree and started teaching at a local college.

When Laura was in third grade, LaRita became very ill, suffering extreme joint pain that did not lessen with treatment. After two years, in 1995, doctors finally diagnosed her condition as psoriatic arthritis, but very little could be done to manage her chronic pain, which ultimately became so severe that LaRita was unable to function. "Life got ugly, and very difficult," says LaRita, who before then had assumed that nearly every illness in today's world could be treated by a few rounds of antibiotics. Family members often stepped in to help take care of LaRita, who was sometimes so ill she couldn't get out of bed. Kurt assumed responsibility for doing the laundry, dishes, and vacuuming—all while working full-time. Kurt only wished he could help her get well. "It's frustrating, the feeling of not being able to do anything about it," he says. "She's trying to get better, and the doctor was trying to get her better. I just had to watch and hope they were doing the right things." They both agree, "That was a difficult time for us."

LaRita had to find a "new normal" by seeing a counselor who specialized in chronic pain and self-help techniques. She also had to use a narcotic patch 24/7. "It was like living with an addict," she says, although the treatment was justified. But even finding this new normal couldn't stave off LaRita's growing depression over her condition, Kurt says, adding that they weren't very close during this time. "There wasn't much going on between us." Not surprisingly, Kurt, too, battled depression during this period; he felt alone, overwhelmed by caring for a young child and a sick wife, not to mention their growing financial problems due to mounting health-care costs and to problems with the business he was running. (This financial stress became so burdensome that LaRita and Kurt ultimately declared bankruptcy in 1998. "It was against our value system," LaRita says. "It was something you never think you're going to do. We felt like we were walking away from our responsibilities.")

Feeling guilty, Kurt kept his concerns to himself. Kurt and LaRita say they both went into coping mode rather than communicating. Kurt had adopted a conciliatory manner, something he had learned from his mother, to avoid conflict. His father was a strict man with a temper, so Kurt learned at a young age to be quiet and stay out of the way. Unfortunately, LaRita had the same tendency. After LaRita's father died, her mother married an abusive alcoholic, and LaRita learned to retreat at all costs. For several years as a young child, LaRita witnessed violent outbursts and the physical abuse of her mother. She clearly remembers one incident that occurred when she was about seven years old in which she tried to protect her little brother from their stepfather, hiding with him in a bedroom, wondering if she should sneak into the next room to call the police or perhaps escape out a window. Although her mother eventually left the marriage, the damage was done; it took LaRita many years to realize that her panicky reaction to any kind of temper was related to her childhood experiences with her stepfather.

Finally, things started to improve. LaRita began taking a new medicine—one that was in a different class of drugs—that didn't just treat her symptoms, it actually slowed the progression of the disease. She could function without severe pain. Once she felt better, LaRita began teaching classes part-time again at the local Community College. Once again, she was able to focus on the family's needs as well as errands and household tasks that she hadn't been able to perform before. It was a tremendous relief to LaRita to again contribute and help care for her family.

Compounding Issues Nearly Break the Marriage Bond

Due to her illness, LaRita missed much of her daughter's adolescence—which caused a good deal of conflict between LaRita and Laura, who seemed terribly frustrated by the fact that everything in their lives was focused on LaRita's health and well-being. Once Laura was grown, LaRita says, they both gained a clearer perspective of the cause of their constant conflict. LaRita's stronger, more verbal personality clashed with Laura's inclination to bottle up her feelings, but her daughter's frustration was expressed as anger. LaRita says she later learned her daughter felt intense irritation when extended family members and friends always asked, "How is your mom feeling?" but never inquired about her own well-being. Because the family had filed for bankruptcy when Laura was 14 years old, she also had a lot financial worry and stress, and was constantly told the family couldn't afford the things a normal teenage girl wanted. They ended up arguing over "everything," says LaRita. At the time, LaRita wasn't sure why Laura was expressing so much anger, and even when she did understand some of the reasons for her daughter's frustration, she says, "I got tired of it."

For example, LaRita says, when Kurt's father died, Laura became depressed but refused counseling, saying talking wouldn't help. "Anytime I tried to do what I thought might help, it was perceived as me throwing my personality on her, and she wanted me to know she was not like me," LaRita says. She adds that all the layers of chaos in their lives—the worry and tension with her illness, financial problems, and "my own crashing self-esteem brought on by my inability to work or contribute"—contributed to her daughter's angst and anger.

LaRita says, "My mom's theory was, if I was lying on the couch looking half dead and Laura could get a rise out of me, at least she knew I was alive." By the time their daughter was a senior in high school, LaRita was ready for her to go to college so they could both have some breathing space. "I was waiting for her to leave the house in the hopes that she would be able to really define who she was once she was out of our environment and out from the shadow of our chaos," says LaRita. "It took a while, but she did." In 2009, LaRita spent three weeks together with her grown daughter, something she says even a few years prior wouldn't have been well-tolerated by either of them. Now, she can say their time together is "wonderful."

At the time, Kurt was exhausted by constantly refereeing between LaRita and Laura. He increasingly withdrew into himself. He took little interest in where Laura went to college or what career path she chose. Compounding Kurt's sadness, his father, with whom he was close, passed away. He felt trapped professionally, in a dead-end job. His boss gave him additional, unwanted responsibilities—with no increase in pay. He longed to change jobs, but felt that he had been in his current one so long that his skills were outdated and nontransferable. At home, he and LaRita weren't connecting; she seemed oblivious to his feelings and needs.

Finally, says Kurt, everything "came to a head." He'd been unhappy for years, but the culmination of multiple growing stressors and not having dealt with their marital issues for so long finally motivated him to act. Four days before they were to drive their daughter to college in Florida, as Kurt and LaRita were preparing for bed, he told her, "I don't love you the way a man should love his wife." Blindsided, LaRita locked herself in the bathroom, sobbing. Kurt offered to go to a hotel, fully expecting LaRita to kick him out. Instead, she told him to pretend things were normal until the college move was over. "I was so afraid if (Laura) had any inkling of things between us, she would stay at home to try to fix it," LaRita said. LaRita was livid, feeling that Kurt had sprung this on her at the worst possible time, but from Kurt's point of view, there would never be a better one. "I was just focused on me. I was always the one to keep the peace, but by then I wanted out." Of course, Kurt now admits that he could have handled things differently (most notably, by venting over the years and talking about their problems instead of waiting until things became intolerable), but at the time, he simply wasn't concerned with her reaction.

LaRita told Kurt they had been married for too long to give up without a fight. "I didn't want to throw it all away," she said. She asked him to see a marriage counselor, and Kurt agreed. The counselor helped them realize their problems had been festering for a long time. LaRita also realized she wasn't as madly in love with Kurt as she talked herself into being. They had both been holding in their feelings and not expressing their needs for so long, they never even argued. "The counselor had to teach us how to argue," laughs LaRita. With help, they learned that "debate" is not a dirty word, and that arguing doesn't have to include screaming and yelling. Even so, both LaRita and Kurt were uncomfortable talking about their feelings. "You have to say things out loud you maybe don't want to say, and there are things you may not want to hear," LaRita says. Once they began to deal with their unresolved issues, they gained a sense of satisfaction when they successfully resolved them. The counselor told them, "That's what you've been missing for 20-plus years."

A Lengthy Separation

Still, their marriage was nowhere near back on track. Kurt remained unemotional; the truth was, he wasn't sure he really wanted to reconcile with LaRita. He was out of touch with his own feelings and desires. He stopped going to counseling. On one hand, LaRita was devastated that Kurt didn't want to get back together— although she hoped that in time, he would change his mind. On the other hand, she was learning to appreciate his new honesty, to appreciate not having to guess how he was feeling.

Kurt, who had never lived on his own, decided that he wanted to see if he could handle living independently. He considered renting a place, but couldn't afford to pay for both their home and an apartment. LaRita felt that if Kurt wanted responsibility, he could handle all the things she did—paying the bills, taking care of the dog, housekeeping, etc. She opted to rent a bedroom at a friend's house and give him the space he needed in their home. Their families, who viewed LaRita's and Kurt's marriage as a role-model marriage, were shocked at their separation. When family members learned they were living apart, "they would stand there with their mouths open," LaRita says.

After LaRita moved out, Kurt called or stopped by frequently to check on her. Kurt was concerned about LaRita and her safety, a protective role he had adopted in their marriage that only heightened after she was attacked. LaRita was unsure how much of his concern was real love and how much was guilt. "I didn't know where he was coming from." Kurt says he "still loved her and wanted to help her out." For her, the constant contact was painful. She realized that the only way to give him the space he needed was to move away, although she wasn't sure she could follow through. When a corporate-training job opened in Orlando, where LaRita's sister lived, she decided to interview for it, and she got the job. Although she had no idea how it would affect her relationship with Kurt, she went ahead with the move. "I figured this would either make or break it," she says.

After living with her sister for a short time, LaRita got her own place in Orlando. She learned to appreciate all the "manly" maintenance chores Kurt had done in the past, but she learned how to do many of them on her own—gaining independence and a sense of pride in the process.

Kurt and LaRita stayed in constant contact, never going more than a few days without a phone call. After all, says LaRita, they had been together since they were very young and almost couldn't stand to be apart. She adds that they were not in the midst of a battle over drinking or infidelity or some other crisis, so there wasn't hostility between them. LaRita says her own experience with "a crushing depression" made her more compassionate for Kurt during this time; she realized that a lot of what he was going through was a personal struggle. "I knew what it felt like to not know your feelings, and I respected his honesty."

During their separation, Kurt and LaRita decided together to continue to wear their wedding rings and not to date other people. Gradually, they started dating each other again. They flew back and forth between Virginia and Florida a few times, and continued to talk on the phone often. LaRita wasn't confident that "love would prevail in the end," but she decided to take things one day at a time. They did some couples counseling in Virginia, and LaRita saw a personal counselor in Florida "to figure out how to grow up." In the beginning, she was just waiting for Kurt to say he loved her so they could "live happily ever after." Later, she realized she didn't want to go back to her marriage just because Kurt was ready; she wanted to make sure it was going to be different. Still, neither one dated anyone else. "We both knew we still really loved each other, we just didn't know if we could live together and be married," says LaRita. Their upcoming 25th anniversary only confused the situation; Kurt asked LaRita to go on an anniversary cruise "with no expectations."

Kurt didn't have any grandiose plans; she had always been the planner. "Not doing anything was the plan," he says. His only objective was to stick with his decision to be honest. "I told myself I couldn't put the toothpaste back in the tube. Otherwise, it doesn't make much sense to go through all this." The cruise, says Kurt, was "fun and a little strange." LaRita was disappointed that Kurt couldn't tell her everything felt okay, but appreciated that he was always "gentle, concerned, protective." In spite of their differences, LaRita says, they were able to connect through sex, which made her feel "very loved."

A Medical Diagnosis Helps Heal the Relationship

After the cruise, Kurt and LaRita returned to their homes, and to visiting each other. On dates, they enjoyed family functions or going out to eat. They didn't force issues; instead, they talked about everyday topics that reminded them of why they liked one another. The relationship was progressing. Even so, Kurt became increasingly lethargic and tired and continued to battle symptoms of depression, despite being treated with medication. Sleep problems became more severe; Kurt was so tired, he sometimes fell asleep at his desk during lunch.

LaRita began conducting her own research and determined that Kurt might have sleep apnea. She urged him to be tested. Doctors confirmed the diagnosis, explaining that even though he was sleeping a lot, he wasn't getting deep sleep, which was why he never felt alert or rested. They also learned of the correlation between depression and sleep apnea. For treatment, Kurt was placed on a Continuous Positive Airway Pressure (CPAP) machine during sleep. The device delivers a stream of compressed air through a hose and mask to prevent the airway from becoming obstructed, and for many patients greatly improves sleep quality. This treatment made a huge difference in Kurt's mood, alertness, and ability to think more clearly, and even allowed him to stop taking his depression medications. It wasn't a cure—he still suffers from some sleep problems—but it was a significant improvement. "He may have still had issues with depression at crunch time, but it might have all been more quickly alleviated had we known about (the sleep apnea)," says LaRita.

A few months after this breakthrough, Kurt told LaRita that he was ready to get back together. There wasn't an "aha moment," he says. "I wasn't sure everything would be wonderful, but I thought we should at least try and get back together." They decided the best plan was for him to move to Florida, where they could start fresh. He looked for a job in Orlando, but found one in the St. Petersburg area. LaRita felt frustrated; she had built a new life in Orlando. "But I wanted us more than I wanted my job," she says. And in the end, it turned out that moving to St. Petersburg "was absolutely the best thing for us to do," says LaRita. Both Kurt and LaRita love the beach—and the fact that they both started over in an area that wasn't territory for either one.

A Fresh Perspective

Kurt and LaRita moved to St. Petersburg in May of 2007, when both were 46 years old and had been married for 26 years. They agree, "It's been really good," though they initially feared the honeymoon period would wear off. Instead, they found it to be more like when they first met in high school, when they were focused on the qualities they really liked in each other: his intellect and quick, dry wit, her outgoing personality. Kurt says she was his first and only love. Their common values overcame their differences, they say. "I think we both made a pretty good choice," Kurt says.

They have continued to voice their needs, have disagreements, and follow them through to resolution. If LaRita wants to stop in a store, she says so. If Kurt wants to sit in the car and wait instead of following her around, he speaks up. "In retrospect," says Kurt, "it's better to deal with problems as soon as possible. I went 20 years without ever raising my voice or having an argument. The longer you wait, the harder it is to change." He adds that they are "always evolving," and that their marriage today is "more 50/50 with our decision making." He is happy that he has learned to share his opinion, although he still doesn't feel the need to "make a fuss over everything."

Their daughter, who LaRita says was indeed shocked about her parents' separation and initially blamed her mother for moving out, graduated from college and was elated by her parents' reconciliation. Laura, who became a teacher for deaf and hearing impaired students, had many college friends with divorced parents or parents who were splitting up "and saw what a big deal it is," says LaRita. Plus, the positive change in her parents was obvious. "She's smart enough to watch us and to realize that we are happy," LaRita says. Friends and family say Kurt is more relaxed and back to his jovial self. They are enjoying being an empty nest couple and adopted an older dog from a shelter. LaRita has launched a business to speak and write about arthritis, an ailment that has affected both she and Kurt.

Kurt says a key reason they were able to get back together after a long separation was that each person started to think about the other's feelings and needs, in addition to their own. "It's not easy; 30 years is a long time. You've got to think of the other person, or it's gonna be a mess." LaRita says, "In some ways, things are like they've always been. There is something strong and calming about being together for a long time with someone who knows you well, and loves you anyway. In other ways, we are more aware of the pitfalls of complacency. We never stopped loving each other, but we learned love isn't enough." Hard work—and a willingness to learn and change—saved their relationship and renewed their love.

Lesson:

Live each day with gratitude,
and infuse your marriage with it.

CHAPTER 5:

MILITARY SEPARATION UNITES COUPLE'S HEARTS

Life or death situations have a way of changing our perspectives. A stressful deployment helped reshape a soldier and his marriage, and created an enduring sense of gratitude in both spouses.

Childhood Shapes Marriage Views

Tim Stoner, an Army Ranger and a Black Hawk pilot, successfully commanded 140 soldiers for a year's tour in Iraq in 2007 while providing helicopter evacuation services for critically injured soldiers inside war zones. Maj. Timothy Stoner, a National Guardsman, earned a Bronze Star for outstanding service. He risked his life on many occasions, with four young children and a wife waiting for him at home. But that tough, award-winning soldier was once a heavy-hearted 11-year-old boy. He vividly remembers standing at the front door as his father walked out of their family home in Madison, Indiana, for good. "It killed me," he says. It is a moment he says he will always remember.

Shortly thereafter, a bitter custody battle ensued between his parents for Tim and his brother, who was two years older. His sister was 12 years his senior, an adult by then. While Tim wasn't as close to his sister because of the age difference, he and his brother were inseparable. Unfortunately, a judge did not take that into account when he decided to equitably divide the children between the parents. Tim and his sister went to live with his mother in Warsaw, Indiana, while his brother stayed in Madison with their father.

"I was absolutely devastated," Tim says. He was ripped from his friends, his school, his brother, his town, and everything that was familiar to him. This major transition changed him in a way that left emotional scars—but it also showed him that he could be strong and independent when he needed to be. Since he says very few people ever left his hometown, he now sees that leaving at a young age probably opened doors for him. Adapting to new places and relationships eventually motivated him to attend college—something neither of his siblings chose to do. As painful as the move was at only 12 years of age, the independence he gained helped him complete college as well as graduate school, and then become a leader in an elite group of soldiers.

What Tim took from his childhood pain was a desire that when he married and had children he would do "whatever it takes to make (the marriage) work." He knew he needed to find the right person to be able to "apply that level of commitment." He also gleaned from his parents and his upbringing many positive attributes—perseverance and hard work from his father, and leadership and entrepreneurial skills from his mother. These skills and attributes served him well and gave him a sense of direction in high school and into college. They also helped him become a better father and leader.

Tim dated girls in high school and at Ball State University—where he went to college—but he didn't feel the level of commitment he needed with any of them. Then at a Delta Chi dance, he spotted someone new. "Who's the blond in the black cowboy hat?" he asked a friend. One of his classmates was best friends with the girl, Tiffany Porter Rowe. She and Tim danced together most of the night and then went their separate ways.

Sometime later on campus, Tiffany saw him recruiting for ROTC and approached him. He remembered her right away, and they talked for about half an hour. Tiffany no longer remembers what, exactly, they talked about, but she clearly remembers feeling "googly" about him. Tim walked her home that night, and Tiffany recalls telling her roommate, "Do you know what I loved about that guy? He looked me in the eye the entire time he talked to me, even as we were walking." She says today that she remembers him being so distinctly different from other guys. He was a small-town guy (so different from the city boys she was used to) and seemed "entirely more mature than most college guys." He was always dressed very well, in a button-down shirt and sweater. He rode a Cannondale bike everywhere.

Tim didn't own a car. In fact, he didn't buy his first car until he had been married for a year and a half. So when he picked Tiffany up for their first date, she had to ride on the back of his bicycle for a trip to Subway. She liked Tim right away, but she was still involved with a high school boyfriend who "lured her back" during the summer. Tiffany was very close with the boyfriend's family; indeed, she says now that she really liked his family more than she liked him. And, when the boyfriend heard she was dating a military guy, he made negative comments about the type of guys who join the military, who, in his opinion, were of a lower socioeconomic class. This made her question her desire to be with Tim, but before long, she knew she should have stayed with Tim.

By the time Tiffany realized her mistake of breaking up, Tim, in an attempt to move on after Tiffany broke up with him, had become involved with another girl—an ex-girlfriend. (Like Tiffany, Tim was close with the ex's family.) Tim had confided that he wasn't happy in the relationship and wanted to get back together with Tiffany, but he reminded Tiffany that she was the one who broke up with him. Tiffany thought he might need a little encouragement to show she was serious, so she took out an ad in the *Ball State Daily News* using their code names, his middle name and her maiden name. The ad said, "DeWitt, you've got to get with me soon. Porter." It worked, and they have been together since 1992, when they were seniors in college.

Tiffany liked Tim so much that she called her mom one morning and woke her up to tell her, "I'm going to marry Tim Stoner." Her groggy mom, who had just met Tim, asked, "Soon?" Tiffany explained that Tim didn't even know about it yet, but she had decided he was the one. "Things clicked," says Tiffany, even though they came from very different backgrounds. She was the cultured city girl from Chicago, whose family frequently attended theatre, the Opera, went to museums and enjoyed dining out. Tim had lived near farms and worked on a pig farm, so he knew all about animals and small-town life. Marriage was still several years away, although both of their families were encouraging and supportive of their new relationship and thought they were a better fit than their previous choices. They continued to grow their friendship and love for one another as they attended graduate school together and eventually chose to work for the same Chicago business consulting firm.

One thing they had in common was that they were both from divorced families. Tiffany says her parents' divorce was "ugly." Tiffany recalls several times when her parents were arrested for various inappropriate actions during their divorce. Tiffany's mother wanted to live in the city, and moved there with the children, but her father wanted the children to remain in the suburbs, where he thought the schools were better. Soon, Tiffany's mother began dating, which Tiffany's father thought was unacceptable. At one point, Tiffany's father broke into her mother's house and had a fight with the man her mother was seeing. Another time, Tiffany's father —an upstanding man with an executive position—waited for Tiffany's mother to drop the children at their new school and jumped out from behind the bushes to talk to her. When she would only roll down the window part way, he reached into the car, and she drove off with his arm inside, shattering the window—while Tiffany says the entire student body watched. Ultimately, Tiffany's father won the bitter custody battle, in which Tiffany and her brother were forced to testify that they wanted to move back home to attend their previous school and be near their friends. It wasn't easy—Tiffany's father was a single parent in a neighborhood where divorce was very rare, and her mother was never allowed in the house (although the children maintained a good relationship with her). In fact, her parents had no communication until about 20 years later, at her brother's wedding. "It was so nasty that I remember thinking I never want that for my kids," says Tiffany. Like Tim, Tiffany's childhood experiences made her more serious about a marriage commitment.

Tiffany's parents, who finally decided to let bygones be bygones (these days, says Tiffany, they are "very good friends," and even celebrate holidays together with the whole family), encouraged Tiffany's and Tim's relationship. They admired the fact that Tim was a hard worker and involved in the military. Her father and grandfather were military men, and their opinion of Tim grew even higher as he progressed into Army Ranger School, a two-month long, combat leadership course. Training to become an Army Ranger is particularly grueling, with only about 20 percent of those who start graduating from all training phases. Those who make it may lose up to 30 percent of their body weight as they get only a few hours of sleep and are given only one or two MREs (meals ready-to-eat) per day. Tim lost a significant amount of weight from all the exertion. While he was in training, Tiffany sent him at least two letters a day, sometimes more. She tried to keep his spirits high; she also tried to smuggle flat food to him. "Fruit rollups were a hit." Letters were randomly checked for food, she explains, so if there were a lot of letters, food was less likely to be found.

There was also a selfish reason she sent all those letters, she says. "I was hoping he would propose when he returned." Tiffany was not surprised when Tim took her to the top of the Sears Tower to pop the question in December of 1995, and she began to plan the perfect city girl's wedding.

Flying High

On July 20, 1996, Tim and Tiffany were married on Michigan Avenue in downtown Chicago. A classy wedding and reception were held at the Intercontinental Hotel. Guests were treated to a great band and mini cheesecakes instead of wedding cake. The bride and groom surprised the 200 attendees by secretly taking dance lessons and then performing the Tango for their wedding dance.

By then, Tim had enlisted in the National Guard, but at that time the Guard was used primarily for assisting with natural disasters or national defense within the U.S. Soldiers didn't hang up their wingtips and put on their combat boots then head to war zones like they do today, says Tim. Together, Tim and Tiffany earned two professional incomes with no kids. Life was good. They settled in her "sandbox," Chicago, where they lived for two years. This was followed by a one-year stint in Alabama while Tim was in flight school. After flight training, they both took off a month to travel through Europe, visiting Greece, Italy, and France, and to enjoy the cuisine and sights together.

They moved back to Chicago for a year and both traveled frequently for work. Tim was also commuting to Shelbyville, Indiana, once a month for Guard service. But the travel was getting tiresome, and they wanted to start a family. Both had always wanted to have four children. Tiffany was willing to leave her beloved Windy City, but she didn't want to live in a small town. The perfect compromise came when they found Zionsville, Indiana—20 minutes from downtown Indianapolis and its cultural activities, and five minutes from cornfields, with a quaint, small-town feel. It was also conveniently located between both of their families and near his Guard unit post. There, they found a great house; on the final walkthrough, Tiffany surprised Tim with the news that they were expecting their first child. They happily closed on the house the following day.

They were thrilled to start their family, and had no problems conceiving or giving birth to their son, Briggs, who was born in 2000. However, when they were ready to grow their family, they were rocked by two miscarriages. Following the second one, Tiffany tried fertility medications, which she said made her "mean" and didn't work. Next, they tried artificial insemination several times. They were frustrated that these attempts also were unsuccessful. "We both really wanted to keep going," says Tiffany of their desire to have more children.

Bombs and Babies

After the attacks on September 11, 2001, their lives changed significantly. Instead of reporting to monthly Guard duty or serving state-side, Guard soldiers began to be deployed in record numbers. "The whole thing was devastating," Tiffany says of the catastrophic event. She felt uneasy in the aftermath of 9-11. She declined being in a close friend's wedding in Washington, D.C., in late September because she didn't feel it was safe to travel. As for Tim, he was saddened, then angered, by the attacks. "Yes, I knew it would probably impact me and our family and that I would likely get called out for a deployment," he says.

Tiffany and Tim had always had somewhat differing political views (she being more liberal and he being more conservative, but both ultimately centrist), and Tiffany didn't think the U.S. should be invading Iraq as a response to the attacks. She had to put her own opinions aside, however. Tim felt the evidence that Saddam Hussein killed 300,000 Kurds with chemical weapons and did not comply with United Nations inspectors was sufficient and meant that America "couldn't take the chance of being threatened."

Eventually, Tiffany returned to her normal activities, which meant continuing in her quest to become pregnant again, but their new normal now included the fact that Tim would probably have to fight in a war. While they were making the decision to try in vitro-fertilization (IVF), Tim was notified that he would probably be deploying with his unit to one of the battle zones in which the U.S. was fighting. In addition to the usual stresses of having to leave family, the Stoners were concerned about the timing of trying to conceive a child. The thought did cross their mind that with frozen embryos, Tiffany could continue the family even if Tim didn't make it home. However, it wasn't something they thought much about.

They decided to proceed with IVF—for Tiffany, a very draining process. Every other day, Tiffany, who already had work responsibilities (she was by then working from home as a business consultant) as well as child-care and home responsibilities, made trips to the doctor's office to undergo vaginal ultrasounds. "You get poked and prodded; there is no modesty at all," she says. Not surprisingly, Tim and Tiffany's sex life became very mechanical and unromantic. Things were bad enough when they were trying to conceive naturally, carefully timing their sexual intercourse; IVF put even more of a blanket on their sexual interest—especially for Tiffany. "After being prodded so many times by so many vaginal ultrasounds, you really aren't even interested to be prodded in any other way!"

Worse, during each cycle, Tiffany had to use a needle to inject medications and hormones into her buttocks and stomach several times a day. The first time she had to give herself an injection in her bottom, Tim was on the road for work, and she had to do it herself— no small feat given the angle required and the size of the needle (about five times as large as the one used for stomach injections). The same day on the news, Tiffany saw U.S. soldiers moving into Iraq. So, she told herself, if a man can go into war, surely I can do this—and she did. Being "jacked up" on hormones caused Tiffany to feel irritable and frazzled. Her brother, who lived with them for a short time, told her she became mean. She acknowledges she once threw a shoe, and she had never thrown anything in her life. But Tiffany says Tim never complained, not even about having to provide sperm samples on his own.

The first IVF attempt did not work, but the second one was successful, and Tiffany conceived twins. However, their elation quickly turned to sorrow when they miscarried the twins at eight weeks' gestation. After a time of sadness and grief, they tried yet again. When a third round of IVF didn't work, many couples would have given up. Instead, they switched doctors, determined to make it work. Finally, on the fourth round of IVF, they conceived a second son and, happily, carried him to term. Gage was born four years after his older brother.

As excited as they were about Gage's arrival, they didn't feel they could relax and enjoy their boys just yet. Because of concerns of Tim getting deployed, Tim and Tiffany urgently wanted to complete their family. "The pressure was ridiculous," Tim says. Just before Gage's first birthday, the Stoners tried IVF for a fifth time, thinking it would take a long time to become pregnant again. They were thrilled when they quickly conceived twin girls. Campbell and Emerson completed this picture-perfect family they had always imagined. Tim and Tiffany spent years undergoing IVF, and this period was extremely stressful on their marriage. It was a time when they didn't focus much on each other, but instead focused on their goal of growing the family they had dreamed about. "That period was not easy or romantic, but we did okay," says Tiffany, who feels she was more wrapped up in getting pregnant than he was. "I don't think he totally understood everything I was going through, but I don't know if (men) can."

On the Road to War

Tim and Tiffany were thrilled about their growing family, but they couldn't help but wonder: Would it be a family without a father? Tim was placed on alert status to be deployed to Bosnia with his unit. The deployment was delayed, but Tim knew it was a matter of time before the deployment became a reality, because his skills as a Black Hawk pilot and as a unit commander were badly needed in the field. He wasn't surprised when he was placed on alert a second time, also to serve in Bosnia. Each time he was put on alert, he had to notify his employer, a small technology company. Tim was one of only three directors, and the notices were very stressful personally and professionally. The business had difficulties in planning, wondering if he would be gone for a year or not. "Being a small business, the volatility was huge," he adds. "The roller coaster was the hardest part." The second deployment was also put on hold, but it was difficult to resume a normal life when Tim knew another notice was probably not far away.

For Tim, dealing with the stress of having four young children, managing career pressure, and trying to plan if and when he was leaving was tough. On top of that, Tim worked hard to protect his family and colleagues by not overwhelming them with information, trying to communicate only what he knew for sure. For 18 months, the ups and downs were difficult on Tim, his family, and his co-workers. "I signed up for that, but my family didn't," Tim explains.

When Tim was invited to Washington, D.C., for a National Guard Bureau meeting in the fall of 2006, he knew he was probably going to be deployed for real. When Tiffany, who by then had taken a leave of absence from her job but continued to work part-time for a photographer, asked why he was planning to drive to the meeting instead of fly, he told her he was going to need the drive home to think things through. "It's gonna be bad news," he explained. "It's gonna be catastrophic news." After joining a room full of commanders, Tim was told his unit would be first out, headed to Iraq in the spring of 2007. After the meeting, Tim called Tiffany and told her he had been activated—and this time it was going to happen. For Tim and Tiffany, having a definite decision about when and where he would be deployed was a relief. For both of them, not knowing when he would be asked to leave but knowing it was in the near future had been extremely frustrating. They also felt relieved that they had completed their family before his deployment. Initially, Tiffany didn't think a lot about the safety issues; she was wondering how they would manage the family. But she did worry as reality sunk in.

A change in Tim's mission also had a major impact on their attitudes, in some ways for better and in some ways for worse. While his unit's duty generally had been transporting troops, the Pentagon changed the unit's mission to include performing MedEvac services, which meant evacuating critically injured soldiers who were frequently still in a danger zone or under fire. The pilot (Tim or other pilots under him) would be given a coordinate and not know what he or she was flying into. "It was the first time I felt like it was really, really real," says Tiffany. She was concerned that he would be in more dangerous situations, including possibly coming under fire during evacuations. She didn't know exactly how much danger Tim would be in, but she knew it was more dangerous than simply transporting soldiers. It made her realize the husband and father she and the children really had in Tim. In addition to being a pilot, he would be the commander of the entire mission, so the level of responsibility was enormous. On the plus side, Tim and Tiffany both felt very positively about the mission to rescue critically ill soldiers —who were in danger and who would likely die without the rescue effort—and about the shift from the infantry side to the medical side. "We felt it was not bringing harm, but taking people out of harm's way," Tiffany explains and calls it a "karma shift." It was something they could both completely support.

Experiencing the Grace of Gratitude

After all the ups and downs, both Tim and Tiffany say they were ready for Tim to be deployed. But there was the not-small issue of four children to care for at home: eight-month-old twins, a two-year-old, and a seven-year-old. Tiffany did have her hands full, but she didn't complain. In fact, she says the deployment was the best thing that could have happened to her marriage and really strengthened them as a couple. It taught them to adopt an underlying attitude of gratefulness. They realized that despite their distance, hardship, and (for him) danger, they had so much to be thankful for every day, including one another, their children, and their lives together. This positive spirit is what carried them through the deployment.

One experience that taught them to be grateful was seeing how many friends, family, and neighbors eagerly came to offer all kinds of assistance after Tim left for Iraq. The Stoners' neighborhood, which they jokingly refer to as "Pleasantville" because of the kindness neighbors have shown them, supported them each step of the way. It started with neighbors tying yellow ribbons around trees and lampposts at Tim's emotional departure. Friends and family hosted a going-away party for him, during which Tim encouraged them to look after his family, noting that "Tiffany is the kind of person who will drown before asking for help." As a result of his plea, two things happened: Tiffany vowed to accept any offers of help that came her way, and friends and family became committed to reaching out on an ongoing basis. Offers of meals, babysitters, and lawn-mowing services came pouring in, making life bearable for Tiffany and the children. "My family and friends were very supportive, and I felt very loved," says Tiffany. The neighbors "stepped up to the plate every single day to help" and also sent supportive letters to Tim.

Tiffany networked with a small group of military moms, and she used a regular babysitter to help out. Tim and Tiffany's oldest child, Briggs, was also a big help, lending Tiffany a hand with the younger children on a daily basis—carrying his brother or one of his sisters through the parking lot, carrying bottles up to bed, and even helping clean up Campbell when she threw up in the car and Tiffany couldn't pull over. It was more than a seven-year-old should be expected to do, says Tiffany, adding, "He was an enormous help to me, and I would not have made it without him."

Overwhelmed by the kindness of others and wanting to thank each person who helped, Tiffany quickly realized she could spend all day writing thank-you notes. She decided that keeping a blog would be a more efficient way to let people know how their support was helping. Even when she was having a bad day, she looked for one positive thing to share, or at least leaned on her sense of humor. Through writing the blog, Tiffany became more aware of how blessed her family was, so she focused more and more on the good things. The week that she and all the children had a terrible flu bug with frequent vomiting and a broken washing machine, she wrote a blog post called "Barfapalooza." Every towel and sheet had been soiled, and she and the kids were all lying sick in the hallway. Neighbors came to the rescue, picking up the soiled laundry with rubber gloves, washing it, and delivering the clean laundry into her garage. Laughing at the ridiculousness of the situation helped Tiffany keep things in perspective. "The situation totally sucked, but humor went a long way."

Writing her blog ended up being "a huge therapy" for Tiffany, and reading the blog entries also gave Tim a grateful heart. They both decided they would try to stay positive by focusing on these experiences and looking for the good that was coming their way rather than the difficulties they were facing. "If you're trying to exude positive energy, it grows if you've written it down," Tiffany says. The blog also enabled her to keep family and friends updated on Tim without her having to repeat the same information with every phone call.

Tiffany is not an overly emotive person; she doesn't cry easily. This helped keep her from falling easily into negative feelings. "I made a commitment to go to bed being grateful and thankful for my day versus focusing on the terrible day I had with the kids or the worry I had for Tim. There are some things you cannot control in life," she says, adding that Tim's well-being was not something she could control. "I just prayed that he and his (soldiers) would make it home safely."

For Tim, the blog became a lifeline to his family. He studied every word and every photo for details on their well-being. When Tiffany posted photographs of their children's feet or bottoms, Tim studied the images to determine whose body part it was, always getting it right, despite the children's closeness in age and size. The blog also helped Tim post general replies; this helped him manage e-mails coming from his family and friends as well as his soldiers' families. Sometimes all he could do was post a cryptic message saying something bad happened that they would see in the news, "but it wasn't us."

Other tips that helped Tiffany maintain a positive attitude during Tim's absence include playing music all the time in the house— usually upbeat dance music—removing cable from all the bedrooms so she and her kids couldn't see the news, and wearing a special charm necklace, a gift from Tim, the entire time he was away. The necklace was something to ground her and help her remain focused on keeping the family intact, she says. The kids also made a huge chain of paper clips for every day their Dad would be gone, removing one each day. The youngest kids had "Daddy Dolls" to carry around—pillows that look like miniature versions of their Dad in fatigues. They took them to the zoo or in the car, and took their pictures with the pillows when they went on trips.

Two things that didn't help Tiffany and Tim were frequent phone calls and videoconferencing. Despite their claims to be the most technologically savvy couple in the unit, videoconferencing was something they avoided except a couple of times. It was too painful to see one another without embracing. "I was preserving her voice in a time and space that could not be touched," says Tim. In addition, most of the children were too young to understand why they could see Dad on a screen but not in person. Phone calls were usually terribly inconvenient for one or both of them, but they managed once or twice a week, and Tim talked to his oldest son by phone. The most useful tools turned out to be e-mail for administrative updates and blogs for personal updates. Tim still handled the family's finances by banking online, which he wanted to do to help keep some normalcy at home.

While Tiffany calls the deployment the best thing to happen to them, Tim—who is more cautious with his words—says it was in "the top five things," calling it "a completely positive experience" that was life-changing. "After several miscarriages and going through fertility issues and the mechanics of getting and staying pregnant, our relationship and our emotions were kind of desensitized. This (period) reinvigorated the value and commitment we had for one another," says Tim. In addition to strengthening his marriage, Tim says the experience strengthened his confidence in his own capabilities and his faith.

It also increased their respect for one another. Tim marvels at how well Tiffany performed under pressure, while she is proud of how well he performed at his job. "I respected him for providing for our family and for being a commander of his unit. He respected the fact that I was left behind and had to maintain grace and dignity during his absence," says Tiffany. While the respect itself wasn't new, Tiffany says it was heightened during Tim's absence, because she realized it took a great deal of courage as well as effective leadership for Tim to do his job well. Tim also realized the strength Tiffany needed to have to maintain the children's home life without him.

The War Zone—Anything But Normal

Tim passed his 20-year anniversary of military service while he was deployed, but what he experienced was anything but business as usual. "You're going 110 miles an hour, working seven days a week with no holidays or breaks. There are people there that are literally committed to wiping you off the face of the earth. They see me and think, 'Hey mister Caucasian Christian, you stand out like a sore thumb.' It's just a different mindset," explains Tim. Then there's the awakening of the fear that most soldiers haven't felt since they were children. He vividly remembers being scared as the unit flew out of Kuwait and into Iraq. "As a man, you worry about things, but you haven't truly been scared in a long time. It's a wakeup call, exposing some emotions that have been latent for a long time."

On multiple occasions, Tim felt his life was in immediate danger as he saw gunfire nearby or came under fire while trying to evacuate a soldier during a battle. During these times, he found himself crying and flying at the same time. "You haven't been scared like that since you were an eight-year-old boy watching the green witch in the *Wizard of Oz*. She scared the daylights out of me." When he was in those moments, he says there were times when he thought, "Well, it may end here." All the while, he was thinking that if he died, his three youngest kids would never know or remember him.

It's hard to imagine that a person would describe this experience as a completely positive one, but Tim says the satisfaction he felt saving a life during every successful mission was beyond measure. In fact, his unit logged 4,000 flight hours, 1,200 combat missions, and 1,500 patients evacuated from the battlefield without a single loss of life or equipment. "We were very, very fortunate," he says. This success was despite being Indiana's first Black Hawk unit and Indiana's first MedEvac unit to enter combat; as the first such unit, they didn't have a "play book" to follow with prior unit's lessons from which to learn. They had to learn more on the job.

Tim used some rituals that helped him psychologically prepare for every mission. Before every flight, he pulled out a small black book that Tiffany gave him, which included photos of his wife and all the children and five small flags. He would sit in the cockpit and look at each picture individually, bless and kiss the five flags, and put the flags up in the cockpit for his family. There was a religious and superstitious tone to it, he says. Afterward, he'd preflight the aircraft, put on his gear, check his weapon, load his pistol, and charge his submachine gun. "Before any of that mechanical stuff, I'd go to my happy space. Then I'd walk to the flight line and literally change a hat…and put on my game face." Except in situations when Tim was physically under fire and his life was in danger, Tim remained positive and didn't let himself spend time thinking about the possibility he wouldn't make it home. He says he had no time for that kind of negative energy or unproductive thought.

Despite the difficult workload and physical and mental toll, Tim says his wife had the harder part of the deployment. He admits that he faced a real threat—the danger—but says she was managing four little lives along with her own, not knowing whether he would be coming home "to be a part of that foundation and the growing of their children." For him, he says, his eye was not on time but busy with tasks and the responsibility of getting all his soldiers home safely. He lost 35 pounds due to the "sheer stress of worrying" about these fellow soldiers, who included pilots, crew chiefs, and in-flight medics.

One of the most difficult aspects of his time in Iraq for Tim was the absence of human touch. As an affectionate husband and father, he missed terribly the endearing touches of his family. Tim is a hands-on dad, happy to be home changing diapers, giving baths, cooking meals, and giving hugs. Other than the high fives of a combat buddy, he didn't experience any positive touch while deployed. Neither Tim nor Tiffany says they struggled with sexual temptation, partly because they were so busy and exhausted all the time. However, when Tiffany's book club decided to share a romantic, somewhat erotic novel, she quickly realized it wasn't the right time for her to think about romance. "It was a light that was turned off that didn't need to be turned back on," Tiffany says.

A Brief Visit Home

Tim had one visit home from Iraq during his deployment in mid-February, 2008 (he had departed more than nine months before, at the end of April). Knowing that he still had more than two months left in his tour was hard on the family. Tiffany says her husband was emotionally very raw, and she wasn't sure what to expect of him. "I just really didn't know what I was going to get back."

Tim was able to share more details about the difficulty of his assignment and its risks when he was home. Tiffany saw that he was more serious and somewhat on edge. "I made the mistake of waking him up one night as he was lying next to our son." She says she learned never to wake a sleeping soldier. As Tim awoke, he recoiled and his eyes darted back and forth from Tiffany to Gage. "He seemed to be completely disoriented and on the defensive," says Tiffany. He didn't know where he was and—briefly—who she was. "There had been no other beings sleeping near me in months," he explains, adding that soldiers are whisked out of combat, drop their body armor, and with great transportation get home in record time, but the disadvantage is that there is little time to decompress before coming home.

He was home for two weeks. His subsequent departure was so traumatic for the entire family that he now thinks he probably should have just stayed in Iraq until his tour was complete. Tiffany, Tim, and the children felt in turmoil. When he left, there was a vacuum in the house, they say. "Coming home and reconnecting and reinvigorating those relationships, then saying 'see you again in a few months'…it is an eternity for the kids," Tim says.

As the tour came to an end, they both began to think more about how to bring their lives back together again. Tim found that the children were relying completely on their mother for everything, and he didn't have his usual place in the home. He also saw that his wife had become the leader at home. "It's tough to go from combat commander to, 'Yes, ma'am,'" jokes Tim. Tiffany worried that Tim would come in and "shake things up" in her house, which she had well managed. Nonetheless, although he took great satisfaction from his work, he was ready to go home and had no reluctance when the time came. He was thrilled to be reunited with his family. However, he says he realizes that he made a permanent impact while in Iraq." "Knowing I was taking America's sons off of the battlefield and saving their lives, so that they could return to their wives/children/parents/siblings was an incredibly rewarding experience," Tim says.

Friends, family, and neighbors once again surrounded the Stoners by holding a huge welcome-home party at the neighborhood clubhouse after Tim returned on May 1, 2008. "It was like a second wedding," says Tiffany, with college friends, army buddies, and many family members traveling to attend. Tim received some local media attention from television news stations and the *Indianapolis Business Journal*, where he was featured for his military service as one of the "Forty under 40" noteworthy professionals instrumental to the city's future.

Reintegration Takes Time

Tim and Tiffany agree that they, along with many soldiers' families, struggled somewhat to reintegrate their family. Competing styles and desires to find the right roles were a challenge. "You want it to be so euphoric and work well, but it takes time," says Tim. Sometimes there's so much time at home, a soldier doesn't know what to do. Tim says he spent a lot of time wondering what he was supposed to be doing, since he had much of the summer off. During that time, he participated in several weeks of demobilizing activities, and wanted to spend the time he did have focusing on family and reestablishing those relationships before returning to work. Tiffany and Tim are both "Type A" people, and Tim needed to see where he fit in, he says. When he left for Iraq, the twins were just babies, and when he came back they were walking and talking. Once the older kids got back to school and he returned to work, however, they found their new normal.

Thankfully, the children all knew and remembered their father when he returned—although the youngest Stoner girls hadn't fully comprehended that their Dad was gone. Their older son, Briggs, was somewhat troubled while his father was away, and was sometimes angry. Tiffany took him to a play therapist near the end of the deployment. For some time, Gage had difficulty watching Tim go on weekend duty. He'd ask, "Are you coming back? Promise?" when he saw Tim leaving in his uniform. Tiffany and Tim say they both put the kids' needs first when he came home, so their marriage took a little time to get back on track. "I didn't feel like we had the chance to really reconnect right away, because it really was about the children and getting the family back together less than getting the marriage back together. It took us about three months to get back in our groove," says Tiffany. They say more than anything, time together helped them reconnect. In addition, they realized the need to be patient with one another during the tough transition.

Tim wasn't the same man he was when he left; he says he is a changed man, for the better. "I have much more of a familial responsibility now. It doesn't matter what happens in my career or job; what's important is what's happening inside these walls with this family and their success. The career is a means to their success and not the other way around." One example of how his mentality has changed is that he used to come home from work, spend time with the children, and after the kids went to bed, he would work from about 9 p.m. to 2 a.m. He'd sleep a little and then go to work early. Now, he spends his evenings with his wife. He doesn't want to burn out professionally, and he also values their time together more.

Tim leaves the family every few weeks for his National Guard service and to maintain both currency and proficiency as a pilot. During his weekend service, he keenly feels the silence of not being around his children. "I don't like it; I like the chaos." Their house is pleasantly chaotic with neighborhood kids and their own coming and going to school buses, play dates, nap time, meals, and snack time, and a funny old cat named Misty meowing through the house. They wouldn't have it any other way.

Well, some days, Tiffany admits, she wishes they had more time for just the two of them. While she adores her four children, the parenting demands are at times overwhelming. "I do have thoughts —often—that it will be nice to be able to be just the two of us again," she says. Tiffany says the child-rearing years are very difficult on a marriage. "We seldom go out. We seldom get time to talk. Kids take up so much time; they're so needy. Everyone's exhausted, and patience levels are low," she says. "I look forward to the time when we can go out for dinner or have a cup of coffee easily." However, she views this part of their marriage as just a phase. "If you can see past that and into the future, we will have an empty house with just the two of us. Commitment is what gets you through."

While they are glad the deployment ended up being positive for them, they realize it could go either way for a couple. There are always areas where they know they could improve—in particular, making more time to be alone together instead of letting children, jobs, and other responsibilities take so much their time. But there are several reasons they feel their marriage has remained strong under stress: trust, independence, and a good foundation. "We take [trust] for granted because it is so strong. Fidelity is never a concern for us," says Tim. Even though she has a lot of male friends, and he has a lot of female friends, they have no doubts about trust. Tiffany says Tim gives her time to herself, which she needs. They have separate activities and friends. And they share common goals and interests and a love for one another. "We were really meant to be together," says Tiffany.

There are always the differences of opinion, especially when it comes to bedtimes for the kids. Tim savors every minute with them and frequently lets them stay up late. "You appreciate them every day and never know when it may end. You don't know what is coming tomorrow," he says.

Indeed, the Stoners don't know what tomorrow will bring. With a successful mission under his belt, Tim knows there is a good chance he will be asked to return to combat. He recently avoided a deployment to Afghanistan when another Major requested the opportunity in his place. Because he intends to stay in the Guard for the foreseeable future, Tim and Tiffany know they must be prepared. Tim says he wouldn't hesitate to go back if asked to perform MedEvac services again, although he would have a harder time in a different role, because his MedEvac role was so satisfying. Today, they don't focus on a possible future deployment; they are thankful for each day together and for the renewal of their relationship as they focus on gratitude for each other and for their family.

Lesson:

Have each other's back. Be a team. Become one.

CHAPTER 6:

UNIFIED IN A BLACK AND WHITE WORLD

Even when a couple is blind to their differences, often the world is not. How a couple deals with negative outside influences shapes their future and determines their level of success.

College Sweethearts

In 1996, during the summer before her senior year at the University of North Carolina–Chapel Hill, Brandy Carver worked at the front desk of her dormitory. One morning, Brandy, a psychology student, was sitting behind the desk when she noticed a handsome basketball player helping kids learn to play basketball. Brandy, then 20, couldn't help but be impressed by his easy interaction with the children. "He seemed to have a real connection with them," says Brandy. "As women, we really love to see men connecting with kids." That basketball player was Chris Barnes, a student at UNC who had earned a spot on the school's basketball team. Chris, then

21, was coaching a summer basketball camp for kids, which was held in the dorm.

Chris didn't notice Brandy at first, but later, as he walked by the desk, Brandy—a tall, attractive blond—smiled at him. Chris stopped to introduce himself to Brandy, whom he found to be engaging and friendly—so much so that he was compelled to ask her something he had never asked anyone before. "Are you open to an interracial relationship?" Looking back, Chris is surprised he raised that question the first time he met Brandy, especially since in the past, he had only dated women who, like him, were African American. For her part, Brandy had never before dated outside her race, but she had good friends of various races. "I don't think the color of a person's skin should determine whether you go on a date with them," she replied.

A Blossoming Courtship

Chris didn't ask Brandy out that day. Instead, he asked her where she had grown up and what kind of music she liked. But the following morning, he stopped at the desk again; this time, he asked to borrow a pen for his afternoon sessions. Brandy lent him one, but said she needed it back, hoping this would give him a reason to return. (It did.) After a few more meetings in the dorm, Chris casually asked Brandy what she was doing that night. They agreed to meet up at a dance club called Gotham, where Brandy had plans to go with some guy friends.

Brandy danced most of the evening with Chris, but her friends (who were black, white, and Asian) adamantly opposed Brandy leaving with Chris and his friends. "A black athlete dating a white woman adds fuel to the fire for many people," says Brandy. "But I had no apprehension about Chris whatsoever." She adds, "He was always so well-mannered and well-spoken and had such a gentle spirit about him that it was easy to relax with him. It seemed like we had known each other for a long time." Later that night, they watched TV in the dorm. As they watched, Chris very politely, in his deep voice, asked, 'Brandy, do you mind if I kiss you?'" She melted.

During the next few weeks, Brandy and Chris spent most of their free time together; they felt like they were in a love cloud. Brandy appreciated how Chris showed interest in her day and in her thoughts. "He asked me lots of questions and seemed genuinely interested." They went to the movies, played and watched basketball and went to parties together. "When we were together, it seemed like just the two of us against the world, and nothing was a concern to us," says Brandy. "It was like we were in a bubble." Chris's feelings deepened as he spent more time with Brandy. He loved the way Brandy made him feel about himself. "It was a warm and inviting feeling that attracted me to her and helped me let my guard down—and made me fall in love with her."

A few weeks after their first meeting, Chris needed to travel home but had car trouble. Brandy offered to drive him. Chris's youngest sisters, who were 8 and 10, were friendly to Brandy, but Brandy didn't feel welcomed by Chris's mother. Brandy figured that she hadn't been introduced as Chris's girlfriend, so she didn't let his mother's lack of warmth unnerve her. "We weren't serious at that point," says Chris. "We were still getting to know each other."

Soon, some friends of Brandy's from her hometown of Hickory, NC, informed her they would be visiting the UNC campus. "I wasn't about to keep Chris a secret or tell him he couldn't spend time with me that weekend," says Brandy. Knowing how quickly gossip about her relationship with Chris would spread in her small town, Brandy decided it was time to tell her parents about Chris. When Brandy called home to tell her mother she and Chris were dating, her mom "was a little surprised" but said nothing negative. Brandy asked her mom if she should inform her father, whom she calls "a good ol' country boy." Her mother replied, "I think it's best if I did." When Brandy's mother told her husband of the relationship, he said nothing for a few days, but eventually blurted out, "I can't control who she falls in love with!" After that, both of Brandy's parents fully supported the relationship, particularly when they noticed how happy Chris made their daughter. And Brandy's younger sister, Candace, was downright giddy at the news that Brandy was dating an African American, as she had been secretly dating one as well.

(Brandy's parents did not support that relationship, however. "It didn't have to do with his race. His character was not good. He just wasn't a good match for her," says Brandy.)

While her parents approved of Chris, Brandy's male friends who visited her on campus did not. After learning she was dating Chris, they refused to go with Brandy to an event the next day and told her she should not be dating a black guy. "What do you think your parents would say about this?" they said. More than a few friends of Chris's also discouraged the relationship. Brandy and Chris noticed that African-American women seemed to have the biggest problem with them dating. Brandy and Chris ignored the dissenters—and even lost some friends—but they did not consider ending the relationship. They assumed the people who meant the most in their lives would eventually recognize they were meant to be together. "Now that I'm a more mature adult," says Chris, "I realize these friends were not really friends but rather acquaintances."

After earning her undergraduate degree in 2001, Brandy worked full-time for a year, and then scaled back to part-time work to attend graduate school. During her first year of graduate school, her relationship with Chris matured. They began to discuss the possibility of marriage. After carrying the engagement ring in his pocket for two months, Chris surprised Brandy by filling her living room with candles and serenading her with the song, *For You* by Kenny Lattimore. "For you," the song begins, "I give a lifetime of stability. Anything you want of me, nothing is impossible." At the song's climax, Chris knelt on one knee and proposed; Brandy excitedly agreed to become his wife. They planned to wed after Brandy completed graduate school.

Influences that Shaped Their Upbringing
Brandy and Chris both had friends of different races; however, coming from mostly segregated small towns in North Carolina, interracial dating was discouraged. Brandy recalls there were only five African Americans in her high-school class, and "whenever a white girl went out with a black guy, she was talked about horribly." Brandy says her family instilled messages that she feels made her

see past skin color, however. Brandy's mother, a teacher, encouraged independent thinking and often brought home low-income children of different races. She taught Brandy and her sister to be friends with everyone.

Brandy expressed her individualism early. When she was nine, her mother asked her whether she supported Ronald Reagan or Walter Mondale for president. Although her parents were Republicans, Brandy told her mother, "I want Mondale to be President, because I am a Democrat." At 15, Brandy learned to be disciplined and self-sufficient after being diagnosed with Type I diabetes and becoming dependent on insulin injections. "It changed my life," says Brandy, who learned to schedule meals and medications to stay healthy. She later used her experience to found a nonprofit organization dedicated to helping others with diabetes.

Chris grew up about 40 minutes from the University of North Carolina in the small town of Knightdale, NC. One of his earliest memories occurred when he was six years old, playing T-ball. Although he was athletic and "probably the best player on the team," MVP honors were awarded to the coach's son—a white boy who rarely paid attention during games. Chris felt he'd been slighted because of his race.

But experiences with racism were rare for Chris. He was active in sports and extracurricular activities, and had both white and black friends with whom he felt equally comfortable. They often hung out together or spent the night in one another's homes. While his family didn't have a problem with Chris having white friends, they sometimes "gave him grief" about spending too much time with these friends—"although they never used the word white," he says. Surprisingly, they discouraged Chris from attending a predominantly black college, which is the path his brother took. "My mom wanted me to have an opportunity at a great education," Chris says. Chris decided on his own that he wanted to attend the University of North Carolina to become a teacher and coach. (He later chose to work in banking, because that career allowed him to better support his family.)

Independent thinking was not encouraged in Chris's family, which Chris describes as matriarchal. His father—a psychologist and pastor—along with his three brothers and three sisters (four of whom are adopted) follow the leadership and direction of his mother, and his grandmother before her. "In our household, my mother is the ruler, and what she says goes," says Chris, adding that his father "stands by his wife" even if he doesn't agree.

The Challenges of Interracial Marriage

After seven years of courtship, Chris and Brandy were married on Sept. 7, 2002, in Chapel Hill. They planned a ceremony that would equally mix their two cultures and families. "I didn't want it to be more of an African-American wedding or more of a white wedding," Brandy says. They had co-officiators—Brandy's hometown pastor and Chris's father—and Brandy asked the ushers to mix people in the rows on both sides so the pictures wouldn't look like all black people sitting on one side and all white people sitting on the other.

About 225 people attended the wedding. Naturally, Chris and Brandy assumed that those people supported them and their relationship. The truth was, there were some guests who did not support a mixed-race marriage. One person was missing, however: a close friend and basketball teammate of Chris's named Clyde. In fact, Chris had asked Clyde to be a groomsman. But Chris later recanted the invitation when he learned his "friend" couldn't support Chris marrying a white woman.

Unsupportive friends turned out to be the least of their concerns, however. Any friends who couldn't get on board got left behind. Chris and Brandy simply found new friends. The lack of support from Chris's family—particularly his mother and biological sister, who is three years his junior—was far more difficult to stomach, especially because they refused to speak openly about their displeasure in having Brandy join their family. "In the beginning, it was all very indirect," say Brandy and Chris. His family would make comments to make Brandy uncomfortable. Once, at a Christmas dinner before Chris and Brandy were married, Chris's mother and sister protested Michael Jordan's donation to the local university because the money would help students of all races. They felt the money should only benefit African Americans, and they asked Brandy if she agreed. "They said a lot of things just to embarrass me," says Brandy.

But Brandy didn't engage. "I've never been argumentative (with them)." She figured that eventually, they would see she her positive traits. When these situations arose, Chris defended his family. He insisted his parents were open-minded and accepting. "I think I was naïve," says Brandy. "I wanted to believe they were open, and he wanted to believe it, too," says Brandy. Now, Chris says it would have been better for his mother to have been open about her disapproval of their marriage before the wedding than for her to be indirectly spiteful. At least he would have known where she stood. "It would have been less hurtful to actually hear it than to feel it over a period of years, and to have her deny it. It could have at least been discussed if it was put on the table," says Chris.

Although she felt less than welcomed by Chris's family, Brandy cheered up when Chris's sister invited her to lunch after the wedding. "I was excited," says Brandy. "I thought they would finally accept me and realize, 'Okay, we're married now.'" But after some idle chitchat, Chris's sister mentioned a friend of hers whose wedding invitation had been rescinded by Chris. Chris's sister wanted Brandy to know if he had been present at the wedding, he was planning to publicly object to the union during the ceremony. Then she added, "You know, I was really surprised Chris married you anyway, because I've only known him to (screw) white women." Brandy got up and walked out. "It tore my heart out," she says. Chris added, "My sister has no knowledge of my personal relationships. It was untrue and said only out of spite."

On the drive home, Brandy poured out her anger to Chris on the phone. "I was so upset and angry. I said there is nothing I can possibly do for these people to like me." Chris said he would call his sister, but paralyzed as to how to address the problem and fearful of the conflict it would create, he didn't. Later, he did bring it up with his parents, and they said Brandy had misinterpreted the comments.

"There was no apology or even an acknowledgement of the subject matter being inappropriate," says Chris.

For the first three years of their marriage, these types of negative family interactions continued. When his family members wanted to speak to Chris, they usually called his cell phone. When they did call his home, they didn't speak more than two words to Brandy. They treated her brusquely at family gatherings. "Family has always been important to me," says Chris. He respected his parents and felt they would always be supportive of him. "I was trying to give (my family) the benefit of the doubt in these negative situations," says Chris. But because Brandy felt no support from Chris, the conflict started to affect their relationship. When she expressed her frustration, Chris became defensive, and arguments ensued.

After the birth of their daughter, Summer, Brandy had an awakening. She realized she had been allowing herself to be disrespected, and that she was modeling that behavior for her baby girl. She told Chris she would no longer accept this behavior. "When my daughter was born, it was a huge turning point for me. I needed to let (Summer) know I was worthy of being respected, and so was she."

As Brandy started to express her deep concerns with Chris, it stirred up more problems between them. Brandy felt she had always tried to be "the bigger person" when his family attempted to humiliate her. By now, a decade into her relationship with Chris, she knew she would not win them over. At first, Chris dug in his heels and said he was trying to be a good son. But Brandy persisted. To his credit, Chris finally understood his relationship with Brandy was being severely tested. He realized he needed to change the way he responded to the situation. Things weren't working as they were— and his marriage probably wouldn't survive without a major change. "Our marriage almost crumbled," says Brandy.

With Brandy's help, Chris began to look at the situation from his wife's perspective—and from his child's eyes. Chris wanted to create a positive environment for Summer. He reflected on his childhood experiences and assessed which had been positive and which he would like to improve on for his own daughter. He certainly didn't want to raise a daughter to be disrespected. He also knew setting boundaries and consequences would be necessary for her as she grew older. Chris wanted to save his marriage—but he didn't know how to proceed.

Drawing a Line in the Sand

Because he lacked the skills and knowledge of exactly how to change—and because his wife urged him to—Chris began seeing a counselor to discuss the family issues. "Brandy knew we were supposed to be a team. We were supposed to be on the same side, fighting for justice for all and for our family. I wasn't holding up my end of the bargain," Chris says. His counselor recommended a book called *Boundaries*. The book and the counselor helped Chris understand the need for boundaries around his new family as well as how to create and enforce those new boundaries.

Brandy and Chris also started marriage counseling to strengthen their fractured union. They learned how to communicate better and attended marriage retreats to improve their skills. "Attending marriage conferences opened our eyes to all the things we were missing out on, like how to listen," says Brandy, who felt that Chris had not truly been hearing her until he began to repeat back her feelings. Counseling helped them "immensely," say Brandy and Chris, noting that it needed to be done before they could address their family issues. "The bottom line was, we needed to work on ourselves and our marriage before we could try to mend the brokenness of my relationship with my family," says Chris. "The most important relationship was the one we have with each other."

Through the counseling, Chris recognized he needed to re-prioritize his life. "I had to come to the realization that now that I'm married, and especially now that I have a daughter of my own, the most important people in my life are Brandy and Summer," says Chris. "That means I may need to discontinue the importance of my family of origin to care for my new family." This idea had previously conflicted with his desire to obey and please his parents. A minister friend reflected with Chris that honoring one's parents does not always mean doing what they tell you to do. He explained that Chris's wife needed to be his priority.

When Chris decided to lay down some new ground rules with this family, Brandy remained concerned that he wouldn't stick to them or that his family would "sway him back." "I had felt let down before," she says. But the way Chris handled himself gave Brandy confidence in their ability to be a team. Chris and his counselor discussed what consequences would follow if his family chose not to adhere to the new boundaries. Chris began with some simple guidelines for his family: "If you want to call me, call my house. If Brandy answers, acknowledge her and be friendly with her." But rather than be cordial to Brandy, his family simply quit calling him. Other requests were likewise ignored. Chris had asked his family, "If you'd like to come over, please call and let us plan for your visit." But his mother took offense and continued to test the boundaries— for example, calling when she was only a few minutes from their house.

Because his family chose not to respect his wife, Chris stopped communicating with his family—although he did maintain a relationship with his grandparents, who live near his parents. After a couple of years of being estranged, Chris stopped by late one Thanksgiving to "set the record straight" about why he hadn't been in touch. He said that while most of his family acknowledged that his mother and sister caused the rift, the visit did not help to heal the family. "To this day," says Chris, "there has never been an extending of the olive branch." While Chris is hopeful that one day, his extended family will make peace, he does not regret pulling away from them.

After standing up for his wife and daughter, he felt like a new man. "I had the ability to lead a family and be an individual. It felt refreshing to me that I did have the ability to have my own opinions and stand on my own two feet, and that I could support Brandy," says Chris. "I definitely felt badly that we had been together all these years and I hadn't developed those skills to show her I could support her." He apologized to Brandy for not "having her back." Brandy says Chris did a "complete 180"; she no longer worries about outsiders splintering their relationship.

Since their daughter's birth, Chris and Brandy have faced frequent negative comments in public. Many seem to come from African-American women whom they don't know; "Are you sure she is yours?" they say to Brandy. Or, they will speak directly to Chris and say, "Your daughter looks just like *you*." Both Brandy and Chris say the tone is usually antagonistic. After discussing the issue at home, Chris and Brandy created a pat answer that showed their unity. Now, Chris always responds, "Actually, she is a perfect mixture of my wife and me." After that, the women back down. "I actually enjoy these situations now, because we've learned to overcome them as a team," says Brandy, who adds the response is also a positive one for her daughter to overhear.

Their Own Team

Being more unified has helped them in their parenting as well as with defining their relationship to others. For instance, Summer knows that whether she comes to her Mom or Dad, they will answer the same and support one another.

Chris has learned that a married couple must be on the same team—and if family or friends refuse to adhere to your team rules, then you're not as important to them as you think you are. "Your wife should be the most important person to you and the person you protect the most," he says. "If someone is trying to hurt her verbally or emotionally, you have to stand up for your wife. The sooner you let your wife know you are on her side and will stand up for her, the better things will be." For Brandy's part, she realizes she also should have stood up for herself long before. "I was scared of being viewed as the bitch," she says. Having her husband on board, however, has made all the difference.

Chris and Brandy aim to create an environment in which their daughter isn't blind to race, but doesn't view it as an obstacle. Summer has friends who are of various ethnicities, but she notices most whether people are kind or unkind. She does ask questions about her "white" and "brown" relatives, however. She recently asked Chris if all of his family is "brown," because she sees their pictures around the house. She calls herself "tan" and says her skin is a blend of her parents' skin colors. Brandy and Chris talk openly about skin color with their daughter, and they make sure she has other people who "look like her" in her preschool class and in church, where other biracial couples attend. "We wanted to surround ourselves with people who are open to interracial relationships and who are okay with us being together," Chris says.

Chris and Brandy are open to reengaging with his family—if respect can be shown to everyone. Chris says he will not lower his standards for how his family will be treated. Chris reached out to his father in 2010, and he and Summer met him for lunch. However, Chris hasn't yet reconciled with his mother, who he says refuses to see the error of her ways. While he has spoken with his sister, she has also been unwilling to apologize for her treatment of Brandy.

"Family has always been important to me," he says. "If you're on my team, great; we'll have the best time ever. But if you're not, then you will not get to reap the benefits of having a meaningful relationship." Although it sounds harsh, Brandy feels the separation has been a gift to their marriage. She says, "We learned to look at people from the perspective of what they are bringing to our lives. If you are bringing negativity and aren't willing to make any changes, then we can't afford to waste our precious time on earth caught up in drama, hatred, and stress."

Brandy's parents, on the other hand, have truly reaped the benefits of meaningful relationships with them. They frequently travel to visit their granddaughter or ask to meet halfway for a meal. In the fall of 2009, Chris's father-in-law invited him to his town's high-school football game. "In a small town, high-school football is a big deal," says Chris with a smile. "I felt like I must really be 'in.'" All joking aside, Chris says his in-laws have shown him "nothing but love and open arms," even when he and Brandy were having difficulties. "The fact that I'm African American has not been a barrier to us at all. They've opened up their hearts, their homes—even their wallets."

On one occasion, Brandy's parents even protected them from racism within their family. Brandy's great-aunt was scheduled to host a family lunch but indicated that she did not want Chris to be invited because she did not want a black man in her home. Brandy's grandmother immediately changed the venue to her own home, and her sister (the great-aunt) refused to attend. "They shielded me from knowing, because I'm sure they were embarrassed," Brandy says. Some time later, the great-aunt invited the entire family, including Chris and Brandy, to her home and made a public apology for her behavior during a prayer. "My family handled it the best way they could," says Brandy.

Just as a team practices to stay strong, Brandy and Chris believe in continually practicing their skills to keep their marriage strong. They practice expressing love in the way their spouse would most appreciate rather than in the way they would most like to see—something they learned from the book the *Five Love Languages*. "I learned Chris is more about physical touch, while I value quality time and acts of service," says Brandy. They also work to keep the lines of communication open. "It doesn't naturally flow," Brandy explains. "We have to set aside time to (communicate), and I need to let him know when I'd really like to talk." Of course, even though they have improved their skills, they still have to put the effort in each day.

What they don't have to work on is laughing together; this comes naturally. They have learned to have fun even doing activities like shopping, which Chris didn't previously enjoy. "Now I don't mind it," he says. They enjoy spending family time together almost anywhere. Chris also makes sure Brandy has some time to herself, for a massage or to be alone.

Brandy and Chris have learned to start their own traditions and negotiate their preferences. For example, Brandy's family vacations always included lots of physical activity, such as running or biking. Chris's family, on the other hand, "sat around and did nothing," he jokes. "We vacated." So to him, a vacation needs to involve a lot of relaxation time. After wrestling with that dilemma for years, they now make vacations a combination of the two styles.

A New Chapter

Brandy and Chris developed their most important marital skills through their own experiences—the hard way, by nearly failing first. "Even though both of our parents are still together, we were shielded from learning how to handle adversity," Chris says. As a result of the adversity they have faced in their own marriage, however, they have created a protective barrier around their family that has strengthened them as a couple.

In fact, their marriage improved so dramatically that when their daughter was two and a half, Chris and Brandy opted to renew their marriage vows. The small ceremony during Sunday church service included their church family and supporters—but no one from their original wedding. They chose not to invite any family because they didn't want to make a big production of it; they simply wanted to focus on their vows, which, after five years of marriage, held greater importance. Summer walked down the aisle with her parents and participated in the renewal, which made a big impact on her, Chris says. She asks, "Remember when I was in your wedding, and I saw you and mommy get married? How old will I be when I get married?" Being a protective father, Chris always tells her, "Thirty." Brandy says the renewal was "really was like a new chapter" for them in a book that was nearly cut short.

Through their willingness to change themselves, Brandy and Chris have written many bright new chapters in their story—and changed their family legacy. While much of their story remains to unfold, these new chapters bring them closer to a happy ending.

Lesson:

Our spouse cannot be our true source of joy.

CHAPTER 7:

WHEN LOVE AND FAITH COLLIDE

Every married couple experiences periods of change, some for the better and some for the worse. Many grow apart, causing their relationships to flicker out. Mike and Lynn Donovan could easily have said that their growing divide was too significant to work out. Instead, they say it was these very differences that have caused them to grow as individuals—and as a couple.

Football Changes Destiny

When Mike and Lynn met in a Las Vegas nightclub, faith was the last thing on their minds. But their spiritual differences lurked just under the surface. Case in point: Lynn considers it divine intervention that both she and Mike were at The Shark Club that Friday night, even though he lived in San Francisco and she lived in Las Vegas; Mike attributes it to a chance meeting that occurred because his alma mater, the University of California, had made it to the Copper Bowl, and he was en route to Arizona to watch them defeat Wyoming. But one thing is clear: Whether it was chance or God's plan, Mike's stop in the Vegas club changed both of their lives forever.

Mike was hanging out with his brother and a friend when Lynn, out with a group of friends, was struck by the uncharacteristic urge to walk over and ask, "So what are you college boys doing in Las Vegas?" Afterward, she and Mike wound up dancing together for much of the evening. Mike was so taken with Lynn that the next morning, he stopped by the bank where she worked as a manager to tell her how much he had enjoyed meeting her.

A long-distance flame was ignited; nearly every night, they spent hours on the phone talking about everything from current events to Lynn's eight-year-old son, and they frequently traveled to visit each other. Although Mike's parents and friends were suspicious of Lynn—they assumed that because Lynn was a divorced single mother who lived in Las Vegas, she must be either a show girl or a drug dealer—their fears were assuaged after they met Lynn. They realized she was a sweet, normal woman who just happened to live in Las Vegas. As for Mike, he enjoyed Lynn's easygoing personality, and admired her for being a successful and motivated businesswoman. "As I got to know her more, I fell more in love with her," Mike says. "He was different than anybody I'd ever met and incredibly smart," Lynn says of Mike. "We had fascinating conversations. It was never boring."

The Stars Align

Early in their relationship, Mike and Lynn visited Mike's brother in Los Angeles. One night, they sat outside, looking up at the stars. Mike, who had long been interested in astronomy, noted how amazing it was that the universe had been expanding for billions of years, and that it continued to expand. Lynn, who had been raised a Christian and believed in God (although she no longer attended church), responded that she wasn't surprised; God created the universe, and she wasn't surprised by anything He did. "When she came back with that, it kind of rocked my world," said Mike, "I thought, wait a minute…I don't recall that being taught in

astronomy." In his mind, faith was not based in fact. If something couldn't be proven scientifically, it just wasn't valid. But although Mike was taken aback by Lynn's response, he wasn't turned off or dissuaded. He didn't view this difference in spiritual philosophy to be "an insurmountable obstacle." Rather, the comment reminded him that his previous long-term college girlfriend had "fallen away" from the Catholic Church, partly because of his persuasion. He believed that he would likewise convince Lynn that his more logical, scientific perspective was correct. ("Boy was I wrong about that," Mike says today.) But ultimately, Mike and Lynn didn't spend much time discussing religion before marriage; at the time, it simply wasn't part of their lives.

In the summer of 1991, Mike invited Lynn to join him on vacation with his family in Santa Cruz, where his parents rented a home for two weeks each summer. One morning, Mike, who arrived a week before Lynn, decided to buy an engagement ring. "I decided she was the right person for me, and it was the right thing to do." He told his family he planned to propose to Lynn during the vacation. "My parents were bursting at the seams," Mike says. On the night Lynn arrived, as she and Mike went for a walk on the beach under the stars, Mike proposed. Lynn, surprised and tearful, accepted. In March of 1992, Mike and Lynn were married in Lynn's childhood church.

Exploration Brings Dissent

The first three years of Lynn's and Mike's marriage were busy and happy. Both pursued full-time careers. Mike's job as a software consultant required extensive travel during the week, and weekends often revolved around attending Lynn's son's soccer games or watching football on TV. "We were homebodies, since Mike traveled so much," Lynn says.

"I was a very busy young mom and career oriented," says Lynn. "[Faith] didn't have the priority in my life at that time." But not long after giving birth to a daughter, Lynn felt a "calling back" to return to the faith of her childhood. It wasn't a conversion experience so much as the beginning of a process, she explains. "I missed the fulfillment I got from my faith." Mike, however, wasn't inclined to explore faith. "I had met other people in college who were religious, and I understood enough about it, but it just didn't answer too many questions for me," he says. As their differences over faith came into sharp focus, Lynn turned even more toward God. "It was (Mike's) disbelief or unbelief and the hard questions he asked me about my faith that drove me to discover and learn more about my faith and ignited my fire even more," Lynn says.

Lynn began attending church by herself—the same church she had attended growing up. "I would hear a fantastic message or have a great experience and come home wanting to talk about it; Mike didn't want to hear about it," Lynn says. "That's when the tension would rise about our differences. He was not open to receiving information, and I wanted to tell him about all the new and exciting things happening in my life." Mike simply couldn't understand why she believed what she did. "Not only was it a foreign concept, it didn't have any sense; it wasn't logical," Mike explains. "There were too many unanswered questions or questions that were conveniently ignored." As Lynn changed her priorities and activities, frustration and arguments increased. "I probably resented the change a little at first," Mike says. "It was putting a wall between us." Even something as benign as watching the evening news together led to disagreements and, sometimes, heated exchanges. "When you go through a (religious) experience," explains Lynn, "it starts to change your basic worldview. I didn't see things the same way anymore." Naturally, their frustration bled into other areas of their lives. "We never walked out or drove away, but there could be some tense evenings (following arguments)," Mike says.

Their faith differences put their marriage in jeopardy. Mike became concerned that they had reached a point where they could no longer move forward. After some particularly heated discussions, he wondered whether Lynn would or should stay in the marriage. Lynn admits that the possibility of their marriage ending did cross her mind, but only in the heat of the moment. "You're angry or disappointed—but you see things differently in the morning." As soon as things cooled down, she always realized that they had a "wonderful relationship." Mike agrees: "Once you let the emotion of the argument out of you, you realize how much in love you are with that person and that this marriage is worth saving," Mike says. Even in the face of discord, their level of attraction and affection for one another never waned. "We kiss and make up," says Mike. The few times they went to bed angry—something they tried to avoid—they made up first thing in the morning. "She'll come and say she's sorry and hold me, or I'll say I'm sorry and hold her," Mike says. "We can't stay mad very long," Lynn adds.

One area of considerable debate was how they would raise their daughter. They decided that Lynn could teach her about Christianity and bring her to church. For his part, Mike agreed to neither promote nor condemn Christianity. "I wanted her to come to her own decision later on in life, and I didn't want her to feel like there was only one way. I can't be dishonest to my daughter in that way," Mike says. While Lynn would have preferred Mike's participation, she was glad he agreed to this compromise. They also debated whether to send her to public or parochial school, ultimately deciding for the latter. There, they say, their daughter is discovering her own Christian faith and is active in a youth group.

Learning to Lovingly Disagree

In the early years, Lynn felt responsible for Mike's salvation. In addition to leaving Bible verses around the house, she pressured Mike to attend church and asked him to read the Bible with her. "I made all the mistakes you could make," she says. "I thought I was trying to help God out, but you can't strong-arm anyone or guilt them to believe. It's faith." In time, however, Lynn learned that using these tactics on Mike only led to feelings of anger and disappointment as he declined or ignored her requests. She concluded that she needed to "let him find his way with God without interfering." She explains, "I surrendered. I'm not going to save my husband into my faith. Jesus doesn't need my help."

Once Lynn had this realization, she found peace. She stopped worrying, feeling that God had it under control. And once Lynn relaxed, Mike did as well. "We have a peace about it, and we love each other through it. If anything, it's made my love better, stronger," she says. Although Mike continues to struggle with questions of faith and the need to empirically prove things one way or another, he notes that Lynn's changed attitude helped their relationship. "Over the years, she's realized that my salvation is not related to her and needs to be my own decision," says Mike. He adds, "Maybe I'll get there someday."

Just as Lynn relaxed her stance on the matter, so, too, did Mike —going so far as agreeing to attend church with Lynn sometimes. He notes that this helped to decrease tension and made the marriage "a little bit happier." He adds that it wasn't a huge sacrifice to go: "There were many Sundays I did go, because it was important to Lynn and to our marriage that I would try to understand who she was. It didn't mean that I accepted it or that I didn't have tough questions and express my opinions. But eventually—after many years—we came to a middle ground." Mike also wholeheartedly supported Lynn's decision to leave the workforce to volunteer with her church, first running an online ministry and then working in her church's women's ministry, noting that the work was important to Lynn and he wanted her to be happy. "This filled a need inside her," he says. "She is very content and feels she is doing good things not only for herself but for others." And of course, Mike adds, it has helped their relationship that she is happy and fulfilled. "It's remarkable that he has always been supportive, especially considering it is something he doesn't fully wrap his arms around," says Lynn. "He has always given me the encouragement and the love and support to fill my heart with this passion I have." She adds, "That is a great gift."

"I'm not as overtly hostile to her religion as maybe I was early in our marriage," says Mike. "It doesn't mean we still don't have discussions or sometimes disagreements about it, but for the most part, she has surrendered trying to be my salvation, and I've agreed to move toward a common ground or to explore more than I would have ever thought possible. That's helped immensely, because I'm able to go at my own pace, and not be baptized for her sake or something like that."

It took Lynn and Mike about seven years to accept each other's differences (although it remains a work in progress). "We wanted to convince one another of our positions," notes Lynn. But, she continues, "As we grew older, we realized we were still in love with each other, and we've learned to relax a little bit." She says, "We started to realize we had to learn to agree to disagree. We do that a lot when it comes to faith matters," although she acknowledges that that's hard for two such strong-willed people to do. Mike says, "I love her so much that I can respect her even when I don't agree with her, and she respects me as well."

Although Lynn says she and Mike agree to disagree, she remains "always hopeful one day he might see it from my perspective." She explains, "I have that hope that one day (Mike) will be able to enjoy the faith I have. I can never give up that hope as long as I draw a breath, or as long as he draws a breath." That doesn't annoy or concern Mike. "In fact," he says, "I'd be disappointed if she didn't (want to change my faith)." He explains: "I know her belief system. I know how strong and important it is to her. The minute she gives up hope, there's a problem for our marriage. It would be too easy to walk away. It would be harder to stay if you didn't have that hope that perhaps you could make a difference in this person's life." Indeed, Mike agrees that the only thing that could bring them closer is his conversion to her faith. "I can wait patiently," says Lynn, "because one day it is my hope that he will understand that my faith is who I am, and I hope his faith will be who he is."

Two Worlds Colliding?

How do Mike and Lynn share their lives despite their different worldviews? Lynn says it's a "big challenge from the believer's perspective." For Lynn, her faith defines her completely. "It is who I am; it is everything I'm about. My faith goes into every decision-making process, and I live it every moment of the day." For the things she can't share with her husband, she turns to prayer. But while it may be a challenge, both Lynn and Mike say the love and respect they have shared since they met has kept their marriage solid.

"She's always been the same person I fell in love with," Mike says. "It's done a lot to keep our marriage strong and intact over the years that she hasn't let this become an issue where, 'It's my way or the highway.' She's always loved me still, and I love her very much as well." Their differences do not affect their love for one another. "I'm more in love with her than I was yesterday or three years ago," says Mike. "Our life is very rich in many ways." Lynn agrees: "We have a very rich life together." She adds, "I am head over heels in love with him."

It helps that both Mike and Lynn constantly work to make their relationship better by making small sacrifices to please the other person. For example, one day Mike got up very early to go to breakfast with Lynn even though he's not a morning person; the week prior, Lynn thought of Mike while at the grocery store and spent the afternoon making chocolate-chip cookies for him, even though she doesn't like chocolate. They express their love often—in front of their children and other people. "We don't take each other for granted," says Mike. "We make an effort to show each other in many different ways that we care about each other, we love each other, and we're committed to each other and to our marriage."

Lynn believes they have grown as individuals and are "so much better" for the commitment they have shown one another. Mike agrees: "Sticking it out has made our marriage strong." He says, "It would have been so easy for one of us to just walk away and move to our circles that we're comfortable with—but we would never have grown as individuals had we done that." Indeed, Lynn notes that Mike's "unbelief is the best thing that ever happened to my faith. It pushed me to really understand it and to really know what I believe." They hope they have demonstrated to their children (whom they didn't expose to their religious disagreements) that marriage is not perfect, but with effort, it can be great. "You have the good and the struggles, and you work through them," Lynn says. Lynn, who says she is very happy with their marriage, envisions a future with gray hair, grandchildren, and plenty of football.

Warning to Other Spiritually Mismatched Couples

Both Mike and Lynn advise couples with opposing religious beliefs to take them seriously before marrying, noting that the issue of faith becomes more important over time—especially after children enter the family. "Yes, you can be married and thrive in a spiritually mismatched marriage like Mike and I have," says Lynn. She adds, however, that people with these types of marriages need lots of forgiveness, patience, and kindness—especially when they don't see eye to eye. "There's a lot of conflict you go through to get to this place," Lynn says. Mike says a couple would need to be very strong and respectful of each other to work through differences. "It's a real, true struggle," he says.

While both Lynn and Mike encourage married couples with different beliefs to work to stay together, they differ in their final recommendation to engaged couples. Lynn gives the biblically rooted advice to eschew marriage if one person is a believer and the other is not. Mike disagrees: "I don't know that you have to call off the engagement." He notes, however, that "it is important to work through. We didn't before we got married, and we've gone through a lot of heartache because of that. If you can't come to a common ground, you're going to struggle in your marriage, and it might not survive."

Despite having moments of doubt at the height of their seven-year struggle, Mike and Lynn remained committed to their marriage. "I was always hopeful we would resolve it," says Lynn. They have resolved their differences without coming to a full agreement. Mike explains, "We're all flawed individuals. Nobody in this world is perfect, so it is working through the differences that has made our marriage stronger." Today, they are as amazed at the expansion of their love as they were of the expansion of the universe. "Love is more powerful than all of it," says Lynn.

Lesson:

The marriage should be a higher priority than the children or the inability to bear children.

CHAPTER 8:

CHASING THE DREAM OF PARENTHOOD

Choosing the right mate—someone with compatible life goals—is one key to a happy relationship. But sometimes, unforeseen obstacles stand in the way of achieving shared goals. John and Julie Donahue of Roswell, New Mexico shared a dream, but as the years passed, they wondered if it would ever come true.

When John Donahue was in kindergarten, his teacher asked all the children in his class what they wanted to be when they grew up. While all the boys wanted to be firemen, policemen, soldiers, or athletes, "I said I wanted to be a Daddy," says John. The teacher replied, "You mean that and something else," but John wanted nothing else. John says his primary goal has always been to become a father. John, who has never been "your typical guy"—he's not terribly athletic, and he had always yearned for a sister—especially hoped to have daughters, fearing he wouldn't relate well to sons.

During his senior year in high school, John—who was raised in a Christian home in Modesto, California and who planned to attend Bible school and serve in ministry—developed a crush on a classmate. Later, however, he was surprised to find a better match in her sister, Julie, then a freshman. "I never liked blonds, and Julie was a blond," says John. Also, Julie, having skipped two grades, was much younger than John, although he did not realize that at first. But the more time they spent together, the more they liked each other. They realized they had a lot in common, including faith, values, and their desire to have a family. "Before we knew it, we were in love," he says. John and Julie became engaged on Thanksgiving day, 1985, during Julie's junior year in high school. Less than two years later, on Valentine's Day, John and Julie were married, when Julie was just 17.

Living with Infertility

Although some people assumed that John and Julie were getting married because Julie was pregnant (it didn't help that Julie dressed up as a pregnant woman for Halloween), the reality was they were simply eager to begin married life. In fact, John and Julie planned to wait five years before having children. "We felt we needed to have a firm marriage as a good foundation," Julie says. By their fourth anniversary, midway through Julie's senior year of college, they were ready. John and Julie stopped using contraceptives in 1991, believing they'd become pregnant within a few months.

By May of 1994, however, John and Julie still were not pregnant. Each month for three years, they had hoped for a pregnancy; each month, their hopes were dashed. The emotional toll was heavy. Discouraged, Julie made an appointment to see a fertility specialist. A few days later, on Mothers' Day, John and Julie attended church. All the mothers in the congregation, as well as all the women who expected to become mothers, were asked to stand and be recognized; volunteers gave each woman a rose. Julie stood, and accepted a rose—but then ran to the bathroom and cried. "It was the first time I acknowledged it might not happen," says Julie. For the first time, she wondered if their dream would ever be realized.

The fertility specialist diagnosed Julie with polycystic ovarian syndrome (PCOS), a common cause of infertility in which the ovaries don't make all the hormones needed for eggs to fully mature. With PCOS, some follicles remain in the ovaries as cysts instead of developing into eggs. These cysts accumulate and make male hormones, which prevent ovulation. Because ovulation doesn't occur, progesterone is not made, often resulting in irregular cycles. This hormonal imbalance often causes weight gain, which worsens PCOS. In the fall of 1994, Julie's doctor recommended she try Clomid, an infertility drug that induces ovulation. She stopped using it after a couple of months, however, saying the drug affected her personality and she became "difficult to live with." Also, the medication was not covered by insurance. "We didn't feel at peace to continue treatment at that time," Julie says.

Julie didn't know anyone who had suffered from infertility. Wanting to communicate with other women who understood her struggles, Julie searched for others with a similar diagnosis through an online Christian forum. Julie quickly found that reaching out to others helped lessen her own pain. Indeed, it was so helpful that Julie created an online support group for discussions. In less than two years, Julie's group, called "Ladies in Waiting," grew into a ministry of 2,000 members around the world. "I was getting as much from them as they were giving," says Julie. She adds, "I realized I wasn't alone." Knowing there was always someone to talk to was a great help.

Although John was also a great support to Julie, she says, "He was hurting, too." John's pastoral training, which he had pursued first at Central Bible College and later at Evangel College, helped him to support his wife, but he lacked a support network of his own. Julie says, "At first, we didn't really know what we were facing, and I think we faced it alone, because to talk about it would mean to admit that there was really something wrong." John agrees: "There were times when we weren't as close as we could have been." Julie adds, "John, being the fixer he is, didn't share how much he was hurting because he was trying to be strong for me." John says, "I couldn't increase her pain, even to lessen mine."

Eventually, says Julie, "We did learn to share our hurts." She adds, "We cried a lot together."

While their pain caused some rough patches, Julie notes, "We realized we could survive anything—as long as we did it together." John says, "We know far too many couples whose struggle with infertility helped bring their marriage to an end, but we'd committed to better or worse, sickness and health." He adds, "It made it harder that our dreams may never come true, but I loved her and committed my life to her." While they continued to hope that one day they would become parents, they worked to focus on what they *did* have together rather than on what they didn't have.

Even so, in 1995, as John's 30th birthday approached, he felt unfulfilled. "I felt like an absolute failure in life," he says. Julie wanted to mark the milestone birthday with a party, but John felt differently. "I had nothing to celebrate," he says. "I wasn't a Daddy." He continues, "I had expected to have at least three children by then. I was devastated that (my dream) wasn't fulfilled and may never be fulfilled." He became more and more despondent as time passed.

Complicating matters for John were various health problems, which began during his junior year of college. These problems were so severe that John was forced to drop out of school, despite having good grades. After several difficult years of testing and seeking medical advice from multiple physicians, John was diagnosed with chronic fatigue syndrome. In addition, John had suffered from severe migraines and gastrointestinal problems since adolescence. The pain was so severe it sometimes induced seizures. Despite his ongoing health problems, John was able to work steadily and manage his symptoms.

A Desperate Prayer

Two years later, although he remained committed to his wife, John hit a low point during which he questioned his will to live. One Sunday in December, John dropped Julie, who was working a second job at a department store for Christmas to bring in some extra money, off at work. Afterward, says John, "I went home and was sitting at my computer. I felt the lowest I had ever felt." He continues, "I actually prayed that if I could not have children that God would take my life right then."

It wasn't just that John and Julie had been unable to conceive; they also feared that they would be unable to adopt. They couldn't afford the high legal fees. Even if they could, they felt certain they would be rejected on financial grounds. They were renting a house, they had no money in the bank, and they had just one beat-up car between them. For a short time when John was self-employed and Julie, who had completed her degree in Elementary Education, was a substitute teacher, they hadn't even had health insurance. Friends of John and Julie, who were "far more qualified" financially, had been turned down for adoption multiple times. "There's so much competition, and (agencies) want the best homes possible," says Julie. "I didn't think they would look at us."

Fifteen minutes after his desperate prayer, John and Julie's next-door neighbor called. She knew of a newborn baby in need of adoption and asked if John and Julie would be interested. John couldn't believe his ears. "Yes!" he exclaimed. After John indicated that the baby's gender didn't matter to them one bit, he was told that the infant was a boy. Immediately after hanging up with his neighbor, John called Julie at work. "How would you like a brand new baby boy?" he asked. Later that day, the birth mother called John and Julie. She explained that she was 15 years old and unable to care for the child. Neither she nor her parents had realized she was pregnant until six weeks before the birth. She invited John and Julie to come meet the baby, who was at a hospital two hours away. John and Julie rushed out the door and drove straight there. "We didn't have a portfolio," says Julie. "We didn't know if sharing our religious beliefs was correct. [They did.] We just started telling her about our families and about how much we love children and would love to have them." After holding the baby, who was just 12 hours old at their first meeting, and taking pictures, the baby's grandfather told John and Julie he would call them with a decision.

The Greatest Gift

Once home, they waited—but not for long. Later that same day, at about 5 p.m., the baby's grandfather called John and Julie to tell them that they had been selected as the adoptive parents. Two days later—48 hours after that first phone call—John and Julie returned to the hospital to pick up their new son. Too excited to sleep, they took vitamins, thinking that would give them energy—but between the vitamins and their nerves, they soon felt nauseous. Julie threw up on the way to the hospital (her dad joked that it was morning sickness); John threw up in the hospital bathroom after they arrived (the hospital staff teased him for being a "nervous father"). For John, becoming a father meant everything. "It was probably the best day of my life."

Before they left town, they visited the birth mother at her home. "I was glad we did," says Julie, who says they learned they had some common interests. "She and John both loved Disney, and she and I both enjoyed crafts." They agreed to keep in contact with the birth mother to let her know how the baby boy, whom they named Cameron, was doing. In the years to come, they would invite her to birthday parties, attend her high-school graduation, and later her wedding.

John and Julie were anxious about paying for everything their new baby would need, but their family and friends came to the rescue. By the time they got home with their bundle of joy, they had received 200 diapers, along with washed blankets and newborn clothing, bottles, formula, and supplies. Julie's eight-month-pregnant sister drove two hours to deliver more baby supplies and cook them dinner, and a friend offered them the use of a portable crib. Friends, family, and the Ladies in Waiting online support group, who were delighted by Julie's good fortune, held three different baby showers. "In two weeks, we didn't spend a dime," John says.

California's adoption laws prevented John and Julie from attaining parental rights until a social worker visited their home and a judge agreed to terminate the birth mother's parental rights. John also had to pass a background check. (As a teacher, Julie already had a state background check on file.) "We were somewhat angry at the process," says John. "Others can pop out babies whenever they want, but we had to prove we were worthy and answer questions about our marriage." They weren't afraid that the birth mother would change her mind; rather, they were concerned as to whether they would meet everyone else's expectations. Specifically, John and Julie worried that the social worker might frown on their decision to have John be the stay-at-home parent. (John had been working as a computer technician at a local hospital, but he quit after he and Julie were chosen to adopt Cameron.) This was something they had decided early in their marriage, since John was deemed "the more nurturing one." Also, they felt Julie could earn more because she had completed her degree. They say it was their good fortune that the social worker who visited them also had a stay-at-home husband. And the judge who approved the adoption was an adoptive father; he went so far as to adjust his schedule to help them get approval before Cameron's first birthday.

John and Julie felt from the beginning that it was important to tell their son he was adopted—although they often forget this, especially when a doctor asks for a family health history. "He looks like he was born to us," they say. Now a teenager, Cameron suffers from migraines, like his father; they often find themselves wondering if he inherited this tendency from John before remembering that he has different biological parents.

A New Treatment Holds Promise

Shortly after her father's death in January of 1999, Julie decided to see a doctor to try to get her weight under control and to ask about a new medication, Metformin, which was being discussed on her online forum as a possible treatment for PCOS. The doctor agreed to have her try it; the medication worked well for Julie. In fact, when Cameron was three years old, Julie and John were elated to learn they were pregnant; they taught Cameron about answered prayer. But at eight weeks' gestation, on Christmas Eve, Julie suffered a miscarriage. On Christmas morning, Julie tried to open presents and act festive, "but I was dying inside," she says. "Besides dealing with our own grief, we had to be very careful that we didn't shatter (Cameron's) faith," Julie says.

"The miscarriage was devastating to me," says John, "which most people don't expect for a husband." He continues, "People don't realize how hard it can be for a couple who has been trying for so long. It was 14 years into our marriage, and nine of those years we spent trying to conceive." Grief-stricken over the loss of the baby they named Katie, Julie and John attended group counseling sessions for several months with other parents who had lost children during pregnancy. John says the counseling group sponsored by a local hospice, which was composed more of couples who had endured stillborn births or late-pregnancy miscarriages, was gracious to accept and encourage them, even though their miscarriage occurred early on. "We learned a lot about grief," they say. The tears were necessary to wash away the pain; John and Julie wrote letters to Katie, and they released balloons to symbolize letting her go.

John and Julie regretted that they hadn't truly celebrated the pregnancy; instead, they had held their breath to see if it would last. "I dealt with deep feelings of guilt that we hadn't appreciated the moments," says John. And so, when Julie, again on Metformin, became pregnant again, they made a pact to celebrate each moment of their pregnancy, even if they never held the baby in their arms. They rallied their church around them; each week, they brought a poster to church services displaying how far along the pregnancy was in weeks. Moreover, Julie's job working as a consultant for a home school charter was going well, and John enjoyed being a stay-at-home father. They felt settled and overjoyed at the new baby on the way.

In July of 2003, daughter Heather was born. John was elated to finally have the daughter he had always dreamed of, and he found that his fears of not relating well to a son were unfounded. Cameron is very interested in science, and John enjoys giving him detailed answers to his questions. And while Cameron played some baseball, it is John's daughter who has shown the most interest in sports.

Completing the Dream

After the baby's birth, John's parents, with whom John and Julie were very close, planned to retire to New Mexico. Although John and Julie considered moving their family to join his parents, they decided to stay in California because of Julie's job. But when Julie learned that her contract would not be renewed, they reconsidered, concluding that "God was closing one door to open another in New Mexico," says Julie. John, Julie, and John's parents decided to live together in New Mexico until they got their affairs settled in California.

Although they were thrilled with their two beautiful children, both John and Julie still yearned for a larger family. To Julie's surprise, being pregnant had done a great deal to regulate her hormones and dissolve the cysts in her ovaries. After being pregnant, her body seemed to be functioning normally. As a result, John and Julie became pregnant again. A year and a half after relocating to New Mexico, they were thrilled to welcome another child, whom they named Aidan.

Although living with John's parents was meant to be a short-term arrangement, all agreed to extend it when the new baby came. And after two and a half years, they decided to make the arrangement permanent. All parties realized that they enjoyed each other's company and appreciated the proximity when one of them needed assistance. And of course, the children enjoy an especially close relationship with their grandparents. "We both feel we got really great in-laws," says John, adding, "When you marry, you marry a family, not just an individual." Of the living arrangements, Julie says, "It's good for all of us." She adds, however, that "adults can't live together without some frustration. Times of vacation do help." John's parents occasionally watch the kids so Julie and John can get away, and Julie and John have created a private space where his parents can be alone when they wish.

Coping with Pain

Although John revels in his role as a father, his stomach problems and migraines have worsened over the years, and his battle with chronic fatigue syndrome has resulted in a compromised immune system. "I don't get sick a lot," John says, "but when I do, it gets very bad." To care for himself and his children, John has developed a very high tolerance for pain, once suffering with a severe shoulder injury for three years before realizing that three-fourths of his tendon had been detached. In addition to using some medications to control his migraines and stomach pain (although he refuses to take narcotics while caring for the children), John has learned focusing and relaxing techniques. Sometimes, however, the pain is just unbearable. "One minute I can be fine, and the next minute incapacitated," he says. Julie knows if John complains or yells out, she needs to ask him about going to the hospital.

John's sudden, severe symptoms make it difficult to plan vacations or activities. Once, when Cameron was a toddler, John was driving him to a Playhouse Disney show two hours away when he experienced a terrible migraine and began throwing up every 15 minutes. Not wanting to go to a hospital with Cameron, John stopped at a store; a cashier offered to help, calling John's Dad and an ambulance. Needless to say, Cameron was very concerned about his Dad, who threw up five more times during the three-block ride in the ambulance.

Living with chronic illness is challenging, especially for a stay-at-home parent. It can also be stressful on a marriage. When John is ill, Julie says her instinct is to "run away and keep the kids out of the way." But what John wants, says Julie, "is for me to sit with him." Julie tries to be more conscious of this so John doesn't feel abandoned.

Strengthening Marriage

John and Julie, who mentor other couples preparing to marry, say the two areas in which most couples need improvement are communication and conflict resolution. "Communication is something you just have to do, to be willing to be vulnerable," says John. Julie believes that communication has always been a struggle for them, although they have improved significantly. "I may assume he is angry (when he's not) then react accordingly." Julie describes

John as a "stuffer": someone who waits and waits until he can't postpone a discussion any longer before bringing up a problem. As for conflict resolution, John says it was often "a dance of avoiding issues or addressing them just enough to make things manageable then stuff them back under the carpet until they're too big again." Frequently, says John, the underlying feelings associated with a conflict are not addressed.

These days, however, John and Julie have "changed the music and the dance routine"; they no longer let problems fester. "We've talked until two or three in the morning, because we don't want to ignore problems," says Julie. They have learned to be open and honest in addressing their problems, which they recognize all couples have. "We deal with it all the way through, and visualize how we would like to come out on the other end," says John. He adds, "Some things that are deep and hurtful to me are not a problem to her." But their differences are not a bad thing, they say. "If you didn't have differences, (marriage) would be boring. You'd never have make-up sex," says John.

Julie, who recently worked with a life coach to complete a life plan—something that Julie says has improved their marriage considerably—has also addressed negative self-talk, which she realized she was doing with John and some of her siblings. She assumed that they were thinking—but not expressing—negative thoughts, such as, "You're wasting your potential." In truth, Julie realized, they had always supported her, and she was putting those negative thoughts in her own head.

Sometimes, John and Julie wish they could trade roles, with Julie serving as the main caregiver. While Julie recognizes that John does a great job with the kids, she feels she misses out on some of their experiences. For his part, John says it's difficult to socialize as a stay-at-home dad, because most stay-at-home parents are women. "It's hard to have an identity outside the home, and I'm too busy for other hobbies," John says. In 2011, John decided to return to school to study psychology with a goal of moving into family counseling and life coaching.

"We've experienced really high highs and really low lows in our marriage," says Julie. Realizing their dream of parenthood has been a rollercoaster ride for them both, but one they call "a wonderful experience." With the benefit of hindsight, Julie suggests that couples struggling with infertility spend time being a couple. "Don't focus so much on what you don't have that you lose sight of what you do have." That said, Julie notes, "Parenting is more than we could ever have imagined: more love, more tears, more joy, more worry, more stress, more triumphs, more failures." The fact that they achieved their dream of a family together has made their marriage that much more fulfilling.

Lesson:

Love is sacrificial; create a cycle of giving.

CHAPTER 9:

A COUNTER-CULTURAL MARRIAGE

Not every marriage from which we can learn has endured major stumbling blocks along the way. Some couples have simply stood by one another day by day, year by year, making right choice after right choice.

Phillip and Margaret Johnston, who were married in Plumsteadville, Pennsylvania in 1961, are one such couple. Both Phil and Margaret had never been involved in a serious relationship before they met in college and began dating; Margaret was the first girl Phil ever kissed. Blessed with early wisdom that enabled them to set a unique path, they are remarkable more for the obstacles they have avoided than for the ones they have overcome.

Less is More

Unlike many couples, who make financial and career success a priority early in their marriage, upgrading their lifestyle with a new car, new house, wonderful vacations, or other rewards as success is achieved, the Johnstons took a different approach. Phil, a physician, and Margaret, a retired teacher, set financial goals early on—but those goals surprisingly centered on living debt-free and not accumulating too much.

Arguing about money is one of the top marriage stressors, but the Johnstons don't have that issue because they live within their means and are content and satisfied. "It's based on the fact that we don't *need* any more to live," says Margaret. Their philosophy was modeled by their parents, starting with the principle of tithing, or giving 10 percent "off the top" to charity. And early in their marriage, they had the opportunity to travel the world and see how others lived, noting that often, the people they saw who were exceedingly poor were also exceedingly happy—an observation that shaped their view of materialism. Their parents taught them to stick to their own values and choose their own way. "We learned very early not to be afraid to be different," she adds.

Of course, not accumulating too much wasn't difficult when Phil and Margaret were first married and Phil was in medical school; they were so poor, they had to donate blood products to earn gas money to visit their parents. They lived in a small apartment and saved what they could. But even as they settled into more prosperous jobs, they purposely set out to live a relatively simple lifestyle. They live in a lovely yet unpretentious home in Indianapolis, and they occasionally buy a new car, but when extra money comes into the household, it is earmarked for church or charity projects and given away. "It resists the temptation to escalate your lifestyle to match your income," says Phil, whose parents were raised during the Great Depression—no doubt a contributor to his frugality.

Their commitment to financial giving has kept them at peace in their home and enabled them to focus on things they feel are truly important in life. For Phil, who admits that he has never been terribly ambitious, the important thing was building a medical practice focused on providing primary care for indigent patients, most of whom are uninsured. Not only has this proved enormously satisfying for Phil—so much so that he has worked well past the traditional retirement age—it has enabled him to spend more time with his family than if he had pursued a more traditional path in the medical field.

Margaret, who earned her Master's degree in Education, chose to work as a public school teacher until her own children were born; then, the important thing became having the financial flexibility to stay home with them—a decision Phil supported but left up to her. "She was satisfied at home," he says, "and the kids really liked having her there." Margaret kept her teaching skills sharp at church, where she was later employed for 10 years as the education director. (She later added church bookkeeping and volunteer work to her responsibilities.)

The Paradox of Giving

Much of the Johnston's giving has come in the form of mission trips, which they pay for themselves, often bringing clothing, educational supplies, and medical provisions. During some trips, they help care for missionaries and their families; during others, they provide medical care, education, and outreach services. In this capacity, the Johnstons have traveled to Amman, Jordan; to the Sea of Galilee; to the Republic of Lebanon; to Thailand; and several trips to Africa, sometimes tacking an additional adventure trip, such as an African safari, onto the end. The trips, says Phil, "have given us some highlights and adventures that are unique to us." Despite the amount of time spent helping others, they always feel like their cup of joy is filled back up in the process. Margaret notes, "When you reach out to give joy and satisfaction to someone else, what returns to you is what you wanted in the first place." She adds, "It's the paradox of giving."

But giving isn't just about helping others outside the home. The Johnstons know from experience that giving *within* the home can also yield tremendous rewards. Margaret explains that individuals in a marriage are often focused on getting their own needs met, becoming resentful if they feel they don't receive their fair share or if they contribute more to the marriage than they receive. Instead, she says, they should focus on what they can give. For example, Margaret ensures that Phil has time for singing in the symphonic choir, because it gives him pleasure. (Phil is also a talented pianist and singer, and he and his son both have perfect pitch.) In turn, Phil encourages Margaret in her educational and volunteer work and her gardening to ensure that she is fulfilled.

And just as important as giving, the Johnstons say, is giving *in*. "That's not to say that people should allow themselves to become a doormat," Margaret explains. It just means that both spouses must learn to give in sometimes. "It is not always good to get your way," she says. Giving in didn't always come easy; indeed, Margaret really struggled with this early in their marriage. But she recalls an argument she had years ago with Phil—she can't even recall the topic. She was very angry, trying to think things through, but finally decided to give in this one time. "The next day was Mother's Day," she recalls. "He wrote a note that was so affirming of me." She continues, "He recognized my sacrifice and knew that I'd given in, and said he loved me all the more." That wasn't the only time for Margaret; she remembers several times when she purposely gave in during an argument even though she was steaming inside. And later, she was always glad she did, as the love always returned. Phil shares this opinion on the need to give in when you love someone. "He gives in way more than I do," says Margaret, adding, "He is so generous. It makes it easier for me when I know he really cares about me."

Keep Moving Forward

When the hero inventor in the popular movie *Meet the Robinsons* fails or confronts an obstacle, his mantra is "Keep moving forward!" It's also a good philosophy for those raising families. How many mothers lament the passage of time as kids hit the big milestones—starting kindergarten, driving a car, finishing high school, going off to college, getting married? We worry if we've done enough, looking back at those lost years with regret.

For the Johnstons, however, life has been a fun journey, and they've looked forward to each new phase. "There have been various plateaus in our marriage," Phil explains. "In the first three years of marriage, before we had kids, it was exciting. We were young and madly in love. Being together was wonderful, and our sex life was great. Then, when we had kids, we really enjoyed having them at home. When they got to high school and could drive themselves, we were glad as well. There was a new freedom for us when they left home for college." And when each of their two children married (both in their late 30s), the Johnstons embraced another transition point, happily accepting their new son-in-law and daughter-in-law into their lives. Becoming grandparents was even more positive. "It has changed us for the better," they say. "Being a grandparent is a plateau I wouldn't have anticipated would be so much fun," says Phil. During each transition point in their lives, they say, they discover things about each other that serve to strengthen their relationship.

Devotion and Respect

What else makes the Johnstons' marriage extraordinary? A certain respect that is palpable. "(Phil) has not in our entire marriage put me down," says Margaret. "He's never denigrated me. He always accepts me for who I am." She continues, "It's huge, the feeling of complete acceptance for who I am. It gives you security in your being." And then there's the devotion. "It's a deep-down thing," says Margaret. "I never doubt that he is totally committed to me." She adds, "He has always worked mostly with women, but I never felt that he had eyes for anyone but me…he is very faithful. It shows in his care for me." It goes without saying that the respect and devotion go both ways.

Phil says their marriage started well and improved over time. "It's been a maturing process," he says, "being so intractably committed to each other." Still, he cautions, not every marriage will be consistently happy. Some unhappiness, related to such things as illness or other life circumstances, may not be avoidable. "You hear people say they're not happy anymore," says Phil. "I'm not sure that constant happiness is to be expected or even desirable. Inner joy— yes. Satisfaction—yes. On the right path—yes. But constant happiness? Probably not."

"Our success is not based on happiness or romance," he says, "but on the mutuality of commitment." Also required is a commitment to the personal relationship between the spouses. "To keep the focus on marriage," says Phil, "we do a lot of things together." He adds, "We also have a spiritual aspect that is fundamental for us." Couples who lack this commitment and personal relationship, observe the Johnstons, often find their marriages rocked when, for example, the children leave home. At the same time, Phil advises couples to find satisfaction in other aspects of their lives rather than trying to obtain happiness solely from their partner.

Of course, their marriage has not been without difficulty. Margaret suffered an ectopic pregnancy between her children's births. Then, following her second child's birth, doctors discovered a fibroid tumor that necessitated a hysterectomy. While she had been open to having more children, Margaret felt at peace with the fact that the decision to expand their family was out of their hands. For his part, Phil was satisfied and happy with the two children they had.

During Phil's medical school and residency years, he was frequently away from home; the very social Margaret sometimes felt lonely, single-handedly caring for the two children and missing her husband. But those years passed quickly, and Phil became an active father. When the children were young, they enjoyed outdoor family activities, such as canoeing, hiking, and camping.

In more recent years, Phil and Margaret have had time to work on some of the "finer points" in their relationship, including improving their communication. "For many years, we were so happy and grateful for one another, we overlooked flaws because we loved one another. There came a time when some of those issues had to be addressed," says Margaret. Case in point: Her perfectionism sometimes collides with his laid-back character. Because it's in her nature to make everything better, sometimes Margaret's comments can come off as critical. She now sees she should have built Phil up more often, especially early in their marriage, instead of being nitpicky. She says she has learned to keep some of her suggestions and advice to herself, or at least communicate it much more gently—

or when she is asked for an opinion. Phil also learned to communicate when something feels hurtful to him rather than ignoring it. They are still open to improving their relationship and feel they have more to learn. "There is a great joy in improving in areas that do not come naturally," says Margaret, "or even in getting out of the same ruts of repetitive behaviors that trip you up."

Final Answer?

The Johnstons note that before getting married, a couple must know one another extremely well, and must be comfortable with each other's family, upbringing, religion, values, priorities, and desires for a family. Margaret says she was somewhat fearful of making a mistake when choosing a spouse, and really took her time discerning whether Phil was the right partner for her. In fact, after dating for nearly two years, they broke up for a year and a half, and thought they might not be the best match. Margaret says she felt a fear of commitment and a test of her faith during this period and felt they needed to break up. But the time apart didn't extinguish their feelings for one another, nor did it lead to them date other people. When Phil offered her a ride home from the library their senior year of college, she says she sensed his affection for her and expressed her feelings for him. They began dating again; this time they both felt it was right. Their engagement soon followed.

Despite her early indecision, Margaret says once she married, she had absolutely no doubt that she had chosen wisely. At the same time, Margaret notes that while many couples feel they need to date around or to test their relationship by living together before making a real commitment to each other, doing so cultivates fear and doubt in the relationship—a problem that is often difficult to overcome. "Commitment removes the fear," she says.

Margaret adds that before she married, she didn't know the qualities that would be most beneficial to her in a mate—that his steady, laid-back nature would balance her impulsiveness and perfectionism. "I realized after I married him, 'Wow, this person is really good for me.' I don't know what I'd do without him," she says.

Is marriage meant to be forever? A small but vocal part of our culture—perhaps because of a lack positive marriage models—believes that marriage should last "as long as both spouses are happy and fulfilled." They claim that making a lifetime commitment is unrealistic, and they are pleased that easy divorces offer freedom when things don't go as planned. But those who seek their own happiness first stand in stark contrast to the Johnstons; despite placing the needs of others above their own, helping each other and those around them first, they have been rewarded by a deeper happiness.

The problem with loving someone only for what they bring to the relationship at any given time, explains Margaret, is that ups and downs—illnesses and difficulties—are a part of all of our lives. We can't realistically expect our spouse to give 100 percent every day. But over several decades, a couple who commits to the marriage can experience joy with their successes and share sorrow and sadness during illness or loss. When you have lived your life together, trusted and relied on one another, and benefited from a lifetime of companionship and love, you can't imagine it being any other way.

Lesson:

Things don't always (or even usually) go as planned.

CHAPTER 10:

A SECOND CHANCE FOR THE BROKENHEARTED

A Lifetime in Three Days

Two basic groups of parents have lost children, say John and Kathy Eubanks of Chesterfield, Michigan: those whose child has died suddenly and those whose child experiences a severe illness. The Eubanks don't fit perfectly into either category, they say, because they had to make the heart-wrenching decision to remove their first-born infant son, John Daniel, from life support after unexpected multiple organ failure led to brain death. To have your child taken from you is hard enough, but to participate in that process was, for the Eubanks, almost too difficult to bear.

Other than some morning sickness, Kathy experienced an uneventful pregnancy. J.D.'s birth was also normal. He had strong APGAR scores (used to determine the well-being of newborns) and appeared healthy. After going home when he was three days old, however, he began vomiting what looked like coffee grounds. With

John at work, Kathy rushed J.D. to the ER, where the doctors informed her that he was throwing up blood. Kathy told the doctors that he hadn't urinated at all that day; she was using cloth diapers, so she was certain of that. They ran a kidney test, which showed his blood was too acidic and his kidneys weren't functioning. By the time John got to the hospital, J.D.'s condition was rapidly deteriorating, and he became unconscious. Kathy and John were told he would need a kidney transplant to survive.

The hospital staff leaped into action to arrange ambulance transport to nearby Henry Ford Medical Center, where higher-level pediatric care and organ transplants were available. A surgical transplant team was being assembled there, and a suitable kidney was being procured. The biggest hurdle, however, was stabilizing their son. Specialists were called in; at least four physicians and more than eight nurses crowded around his tiny frame. A pharmacologist and lab technician were assigned to him. "It was all hands on deck," says John.

Although many tests were being performed, none came back that could positively identify his condition. After even more tests, doctors told the Eubanks that J.D.'s liver was also failing, and he would also need a liver transplant. Then little J.D. went into cardiac arrest. Kathy vividly remembers several times hearing the machines buzzing and seeing the staff rush to restart his heart. John says it happened so many times (as many as 10) they lost count. He would need a heart transplant, along with the new kidney and liver.

For two new parents without medical training, they struggled to keep up with new information on their son's status. John quickly realized that even if they stabilized J.D. for transport, they didn't understand what was causing his organs to fail, or what would prevent new organs from failing. A special surgeon was called in to insert a central venous line in the three-day-old infant. J.D.'s medical situation was "way outside their realm of capabilities," says John of the community hospital's medical team, but adds, "Even at a tier-one trauma center for children, the results probably wouldn't have been any different."

After several hours in the ER, the medical team finally stabilized J.D. for transport. The medical team at Henry Ford was busy trying to find organ tissue matches. Surgeons were lined up and ready for his arrival. John says it was terrifying knowing that there would be a second phase of this process at another hospital 20 miles away. "All we knew is they had to get him there. It was just a series of checking the boxes" to get him stabilized, transported, and ready for the transplants, John says.

John went to get the car so that he and Kathy could drive behind the ambulance with doctors and nurses working inside. Kathy was with J.D. when he suddenly opened his eyes before being loaded into the ambulance. "It was a complete shock to everyone," says Kathy, who could clearly see he was suffering. She whispered a Polish phrase to him that her parents said to her when they tucked her into bed, "Spać z Bogiem," which means, "Sleep with God." He closed his eyes.

The medical team loaded him into the ambulance and closed the door. John and Kathy waited behind, but the ambulance didn't move for what seemed like a long time. Eventually, they opened the door. J.D. had experienced another cardiac arrest, and the team had been performing CPR on him. He wasn't stable enough to move. They brought J.D. back into the hospital and placed him on machines to oxygenate his blood and help him breathe. Doctors told Kathy and John that he now had no brain activity. "Now, you need to make some decisions," a doctor told them. "The way it was put to us," says John, "is that the continuous cascading systemic failures will only move to other organs. What's left? You don't call up the hospital and say, 'Send me up a heart, two lungs, two kidneys and a brain.'"

Kathy calls the fact that she and John had attended a marriage-encounter weekend retreat the year prior "divine intervention." There, they had discussed how they defined life and living and whether they would want life support used on themselves. "Fortunately, we had those conversations. We knew what we thought constituted life and what we would want done. So we told them to discontinue life support," says Kathy. Still, Kathy says, they were hoping for a miracle when life-support machines were removed, although they knew the odds were very low. Within a matter of minutes, J.D. was gone. Kathy regrets now that she did not insist on being with J.D. when he died. The nurses wrapped him up in a blanket and brought him to his parents. He still had some tubes hanging from his body, but he looked so peaceful. "He was remarkably very beautiful," says John. A photographer took pictures, which they now treasure, more than 18 years later.

The hospital staff was surprisingly shaken up, John says. "Nurses with 25 years of experience were just bawling. The kind-hearted Vietnamese physician was beside himself and said he was going home to hug his children," says John, who adds that he was in shock. "It was like being in a war with everyone firing over your head, and you're trying to keep your head down." The experience of going home from the hospital without their baby in their arms was unimaginably painful.

The next day, Kathy's parents drove them to the coroner's office, where they had to identify their son's body. Then, they planned a service for immediate family and close friends, including a funeral Mass. An autopsy was conducted, but John says it was "completely botched" with erroneous information and missing major details, such as the femoral shunt (an incision in the leg in which to insert a tube). "There was a complete and utter dereliction of duty," John says. The Eubanks struggled just to get the copy of the coroner's report, eventually filing a lawsuit against the coroner's office and enlisting the help of a local TV station to obtain it. The Eubanks shared the coroner's diagnosis of pyloric stenosis with nearly 50 doctors and were told that the diagnosis was not consistent with all that occurred.

Obtaining a proper diagnosis was so important to John and Kathy because they wanted to have more children, but were unsure whether their experience with J.D. was likely to repeat itself. The medical team suggested a bacterial or viral infection was a possibility, but neither Kathy's blood nor J.D.'s blood tested positive for either. A genetic disorder, perhaps related to the metabolism of glucose, was therefore a more likely possibility. Visits to a geneticist were inconclusive; however, John says, they were told that most genetically linked mortalities are male dominated and located on the Y chromosome. If it was a genetic disorder, subsequent male children would have a 50-percent chance of having the same problem.

How They Grieved

Kathy was lactating, and her hormones were causing her to crave contact with her baby. "It was just devastating," says John. "Her milk was coming in. All the hormonal processes were taking place. It wasn't long after that we were in a restaurant, and she heard a baby crying." Kathy continues the story, "The next thing I know my shirt was completely saturated. It was very difficult." And there were other stressors: Kathy had quit her job to be a full-time mother. John's mother, who had fallen on hard times, was living with them in their 700-square-foot home. They had nearly finished the stressful process of building a new home that would accommodate his mother and their child, and were preparing to move when J.D. was born. Two weeks after burying J.D., their house sold, and they had to move in with Kathy's parents while their new house was completed. "It was just chaos," says Kathy, who missed her old home, her old neighborhood, her church, her job, and of course, her baby. Friends and family congregated around her to offer their support. "A lot of people came in and sort of circled the wagons around Kathy," says John. Kathy says one of the nicest things someone said was, "What was your son's name?" It was a simple question, but the fact that someone asked about him touched her heart.

For John, however, things were different. When John, who sells technical products to a global market, returned to work, his co-workers did not know how to handle his loss, and many were "downright indifferent." Some asked him how his wife was, but not how he was. Many didn't even acknowledge his son's death. "You don't have to absolutely empathize, but it's not business as usual," John says. "Ignoring it is worse." It's a classic American male tendency to expect people to "get back in the saddle" and move on, but for about six months, he just couldn't. John says he understood intellectually that he and Kathy didn't have a long history with their child, and that it wasn't the same as losing your 25-year-old son, "but they don't consider the lasting effects and the whole issue we were struggling with about whether to have another child. The whole mystery behind it was not revealed. That made it worse." Interestingly, in John's experience, the people he had formerly considered most compassionate didn't speak to John about J.D.'s death, but a man he had always thought of as a "jerk" invited John to talk about it, adding that his own son had died and he had "been there". Their work relationship changed for the better.

At home, Kathy and John's marriage became strained. Kathy stopped sleeping at night. Depressed and frequently in tears, Kathy isolated herself, turning inward; John didn't know how to react. John noticed her behavior, but "just stopped doing anything." "Where initially he would have put his hand on my shoulder, that stopped," says Kathy. "He became cold and distant. We shared the same bed, but we might as well not have. We could go through whole meals and not say a word." Sometimes they turned to alcohol to numb their pain. "There were nights where one of us would get toasted and the other wouldn't. We'd trade off," Kathy says. The problem, Kathy says now, was that they lacked compassion for one another. "We were nasty," she says. "We were short or completely apathetic." She explains, "He was grieving in his way; I was grieving in my way."

About nine months after J.D. died, John came home from work, only to find Kathy crying again. "I don't know how much more of this I can take," he told her. John still loved Kathy, but it was difficult for him seeing her in such pain. "I remember for the year after, going to church every Sunday and listening to the babies cry. I could see it in her face. We had to leave every time. I don't know how many times this happened—as soon as a baby started crying, boom, we were out of there." While John simply meant that it was hard for him to see her suffering, Kathy interpreted his comment to mean, "If you don't get happy, I will leave." After that, everything John said had a hidden connotation in Kathy's mind. She became convinced he was going to leave her. "In my mind, divorce was the inevitable conclusion," Kathy says. But then it occurred to Kathy that the last thing J.D. would ever want would be to have his parents split up because of him.

After prayer and soul-searching, Kathy decided to confront her husband. "Are you planning to divorce me?" she asked. John was taken by surprise. "No way," he said. That night, they talked, cried, and decided they needed to start grieving together. Kathy says, "I realized that the only person who could understand losing our son and the decision we had to make was John." The next day, they visited the cemetery where J.D. was buried. On the way, John got pulled over for speeding. "We had these pathetic grocery-store flowers and terrible expressions on our faces. I milked it a little and told the officer we were going to the cemetery where we had just buried our son," says John. The officer let them go. That day served as a turning point for them as they became more unified in their suffering.

John and Kathy tried going to support groups, but felt like no one understood exactly what they were going through. Attending one group that was connected to a local church was like going through the funeral all over again, but with more grieving parents. John told Kathy, "If we end up like these people, I'm gonna put a bullet in my brain." They decided not to return, but sought God's help, saying "You've got to help us through this thing." Faith was particularly important in John and Kathy's attempts to overcome the anger they felt as they moved through the phases of grief. "I was angry for a long time," Kathy says. "Half my brain was in a lock, and the other half was saying there's a bigger purpose to this that I don't understand. I'm angry about it but I'm going to trust and fight through this until I can understand it." She adds, "I do understand it now because I see all the good that's come out of it." For his part, John and his Lord had some difficult times. "We've had our down and outs. I don't really think I was the type that said, 'Blast you, God, for doing this.' It was more, 'What do I do next?' But I had my temper tantrums." John says he had many conversations with God and he concluded, "I know we've already had our time in the barrel. I've given my son, and you've given yours. We're even. It's not going to happen again." In that moment, John says, he decided things were going to turn out alright. They started to look toward the future "because living in the present felt like a prison," John says. They scheduled a backpack trip with close friends. They wrote a ten-year plan of places they wanted to go and things they wanted to do. They decided to invite close friends and family over and begin entertaining again, "even if we cry all night," says Kathy.

Assessing their Past and Future

As they looked forward, John and Kathy made it a point to remember the happiness they had felt in the first five years of their marriage. "We had a blast," Kathy says. They recalled, too, the reasons they fell in love. John was 24 when he met Kathy, then 25, at a bar in Detroit in November of 1987. Kathy, with her big 80s hair, was with a group celebrating her brother's 21st birthday. John was interested, but assumed she was with one of the guys there; she let him know she was single. He was "drop-dead gorgeous," she says. "The cutest guy you've ever seen." John found Kathy to be "cute and bubbly with a wonderful personality." They exchanged information and went out a couple of weeks later. "I could just tell he was a good guy. He was gentle and calm in his speech and manner." John was impressed with Kathy's intelligence, and with her job as the director of an ultrasound lab at an eye institute. They had a common interest in science, as his background was in biochemistry and chemical engineering. They also both enjoyed outdoor activities, including skiing and camping.

After only a few months of dating, John told Kathy he wanted to marry her, but Kathy felt they hadn't known each other long enough. John said he would wait until she was ready. A few months later, he again asked her to marry him; she responded the same way as before. But when, after nearly a year of dating, John proposed a third time, Kathy finally agreed. John's marriage proposal showed his sense of humor; he knelt down with his grandmother's ring in one hand and a 19-inch color TV in the other arm. Kathy's practical side was likewise revealed in her response; she was probably more excited about the TV since at the time she had only a 14-inch black and white set. They were married in February of 1989, and the early years of their marriage were incredibly happy times.

As John and Kathy recalled their history, they realized their relationship was something worth saving. This was perhaps especially so for Kathy, who had been physically and sexually abused by her first husband for two years before escaping with only the clothes on her back. She had no idea when she married him that he was a controlling, drug-abusing gambler, even though they dated three years while she was in college. After their wedding, her first husband had changed abruptly, abusing her on a regular basis and even controlling how much food she was allowed to eat. He was meticulous about injuring her in places that were not visible—her chest, back or under her hair—so her family and friends did not suspect abuse, and she was too proud to reach out for help right away. Eventually, with help from a battered-women's shelter, a supportive family, law enforcement, and extensive counseling, she regained her life. (Later, Kathy even became an expert on identifying controlling men and had volunteered regularly at the shelter that helped her. Once, she helped a girlfriend's sister escape abuse, because she saw the signs before any of the girl's family did.) Of course, Kathy had been cautious when she started dating John, but concluded, "John wasn't at all controlling and not the slightest bit jealous." For his part, John was patient with Kathy, understanding she had been through a difficult trauma and needed time to heal. He didn't mind waiting to get married until Kathy felt she was ready to take that chance again.

"We went through so much," says Kathy, but John and Kathy still envisioned a happy family for themselves. After J.D.'s death, "We wondered, do we have a right to do this to another child? We asked ourselves, 'Do we have the strength to deal with this again?'" Finally, they decided that they did. They considered adoption but ultimately decided that they really wanted to have a child of their own. After prayer, they decided to "leave it in God's hands." At the same time, they decided to "do the best we can to have all females." They studied for hours in medical libraries to learn techniques involving timing, temperatures, positions, and motility rates.

They had no difficulty conceiving. ("When he *looks* at me I get pregnant," says Kathy.) Finding a high-risk OB was a real challenge, however. Because of their history of losing a child and litigation against the coroner, few doctors would go near them, they say. But when they did become pregnant, they had found an excellent doctor who knew all of their history. He asked the Eubanks if they would like to learn the sex of their child, but they declined. They said, if it's a boy, you can make all the needed preparations; but we don't want to spend nine months worrying, possibly to the detriment of the baby. Amazingly, Kathy had a remarkably peaceful pregnancy without worry. "I'm sure that was divine." They prayed, usually daily. John says, "I learned a long time ago, it doesn't make sense to pray the same thing over and over. We made our initial prayer and left it at that. We put the pregnancy in God's hands, and we prayed for wisdom, patience and other things."

Four years after J.D.'s death, they gave birth to a healthy baby girl, Jacquelyn; they felt relieved and blessed. Two years later, they were overjoyed by the arrival of a second healthy little girl, whom they named Kylee. And they were pleasantly surprised seven years after that when they became pregnant with Kristyn, who is now four years old. Kristyn says she sometimes plays with her little brother, J.D., whom she sees in a picture on the wall. Sometimes one of the girls has a dream of the whole family, including J.D. But for the girls, "It's ancient history," says Kathy. For John and Kathy, however, J.D.'s memory is still alive and well. When Kathy recently heard a friend's daughter had obtained her driver's license, she realized J.D. would have been driving. When they saw the eighth-grade class graduation, they knew he would have been among them. When John watched high-school boys playing baseball, John thought, "That could have been him out there."

How their Trials Improved their Marriage

While the loss of their son was devastating, Kathy says it also affected them in a positive way. "The fact that we weathered that storm, I know it's made our marriage 100 times stronger." John agrees—there won't be much worse than that to face in life, other than facing their own mortality. The experience also made them realize how fragile a marriage can be—and with three children, adds Kathy, it's even more of a challenge to keep it strong—unless it is made a priority and worked on daily. "The commitment is there, but we know we have to do the work," says Kathy. She adds, "Sometimes it's not work; it's easy and fun."

Before they get up each morning, they take a few minutes together, sometimes scratching the other's back or saying a prayer together. And throughout the day, they make small efforts to please the other—he'll unload the dishwasher for her or she'll fix the toilet for him. Whoever's up and about offers to bring a snack or drink to the one watching TV. "We make it a point to do at least one nice thing every day for the other person," Kathy says. Admittedly, that's not always easy for Kathy, who bears the brunt of getting up at night to care for their youngest, who has sleeping difficulties. But John cuts Kathy some additional slack if she's short-tempered or cranky, taking on additional responsibilities during the day. "He's more patient, because he knows I'm only irritable because I haven't slept." But even when there is household stress, they keep their marriage number one. "If our marriage is not a priority, everything else loses —our sex life loses, our kids lose, we lose," says Kathy.

John says there's no magic book to figuring out marriage; you have to do it on your own. Kathy adds that books like *Men are from Mars, Women are from Venus* don't explain her husband very well. "He doesn't necessarily think like other men. I only need to know how he works. The way he works isn't in any book." They agree that trial and error and studying your partner early in your marriage is the best way to learn what pleases your spouse. Then, says John, just be interested. "Put the energy and emotional energy into it. Is it more energy than we anticipated? Absolutely...but well worth it."

Their son's death also has also affected how Kathy and John parent their daughters. "I know I am much more protective of my children and much more involved in their lives," Kathy says. "I don't think either one of us ever takes a minute of their being in our lives for granted." In parenting, John and Kathy are very unified. "You can't undermine one another, or the kids will divide and conquer," says John. Kathy adds, "We don't always agree, but we talk without the kids there." Often, when John and Kathy do disagree, it's about something deeper than what they are arguing about, so they try to be reasonable and listen to what is really important to the other.

For John, selecting the right mate was key. His father, who died when John was only 14, told him to find a wife who would work with him rather than against him—a quality he found in Kathy. He observes that a lot of people know they are dating someone who opposes them, but they think they can change them after the marriage. "It's not the case." Selecting the right mate was key for Kathy as well. After Kathy divorced her first husband, her mother urged her to make a long list of all the things she wanted in a husband and tuck it away. (Her mother had also made such a list, and had celebrated more than 50 years of happy matrimony with Kathy's father, the man who met her criteria.) For Kathy, those things included being a man of God who prioritized his wife and family. Five years into her marriage to John, Kathy found that list, and realized John was everything she had hoped for.

The Eubanks talk to their daughters about making good choices. They make time for family dinners most nights, during which the girls are asked to say at least one nice thing to one another. They model forgiveness and talk of second chances. The older girls even know a little of Kathy's first marriage, and are taught to never tolerate any abusive behavior—something John and Kathy shared with them for safety's sake, in case Kathy's ex reappeared. (Seven years after her divorce, when Kathy was already married to John, her ex showed up at her workplace, looking for her. Fortunately, Kathy looked completely different—no longer the almost anorexic long-haired young woman he had known, she had added some curves and shortened and permed her hair—so he didn't recognize her. It was many years before Kathy stopped fearing he was around the next corner.) For Kathy, that first marriage seems like a different life entirely, in which she was a completely different person; she hopes her daughters will learn that "even if you do something stupid in your life, that doesn't have to be the end. There can be some redemption for all of us." Perhaps most importantly, the Eubanks teach their daughters to make that list of everything they want in a husband. Kathy tells them if they find a man like their father, "Don't miss it."

Kathy used the failure of her first marriage as the impetus for reshaping her own life and for setting much higher expectations with respect to how others should treat her. And yet, even after making all the right choices, Kathy and John faced tragedy, with J.D.'s death occurring during what should have been a joyous time. Fortunately, Kathy and John used this tragedy as another turning point that, after a lengthy healing process, enabled them to focus on the good in their marriage and in their lives. Now blessed with more children, they share the knowledge that we all face turning points, and we all must decide how to move forward. It takes a discerning heart to see the opportunities—even the blessings—that bloom from heartache.

Lesson:

Adversity is not a killer–it can be a strengthener.

CHAPTER 11:

FOR BETTER OR FOR WORSE

In movies and soap operas, people in comas awaken suddenly, while holding their soul mate's hand. Within days, they are back to good health, resuming their lives. Patty and Paul Jerde wish real life was more like that. In their case, a tragic accident changed their lives forever—but it also brought them closer together.

Easy Street

When the Jerdes shared their wedding vows in September of 1997, they gave little thought to their spoken promise "for better or worse, in sickness and in health." They, like most couples, thought one of them might get sick when they were old, but they never considered one of them could become disabled or completely dependent in the near future. Thinking about a young, vibrant person being killed or disabled would have seemed morbid during a wedding celebration—even if that celebration took place on the day of Princess Diana's funeral, as the Jerdes' wedding did.

More than 10 years later, Patty and Paul remained well-matched and happy. At 43, the silver-haired Paul had advanced his career to become creative director at an ad agency, demonstrating his artistic skills as a graphic designer. Meanwhile, Patty, six months his junior, enjoyed her work in communications and PR. Both were elated to have their son, Buzz, enter their lives in 2002, especially after three years of trying to become pregnant and suffering a miscarriage prior to Buzz's birth. Buzz's wavy, golden locks gave him a fun-loving look to match his personality. The picture-perfect family members— each with striking blue eyes and fair skin—felt fortunate to have each other.

While Paul was focused on his career and professional associations, Patty enjoyed her job, running, meeting with her book club, and spending time with her five siblings and mother, all of whom lived nearby. In some ways, because of their careers and activities, they lived separate lives during the week. On weekends, they connected as a family, going to Buzz's T-ball games, out to eat, or playing at home.

Their low-key lifestyle differed from the wild and crazy one they shared when they first met at Dick's Last Resort, where they both had waited tables for years. Paul and Patty had given up drinking before getting married. Paul went sober first; Patty was more reluctant to do so. She just couldn't imagine having fun without alcohol. But after a rough patch, Paul made it clear that the only way the relationship would work was if Patty followed his lead on the matter. After going cold turkey, Patty found sobriety freeing and exhilarating. Both Paul and Patty realized how much alcohol had held them back in their relationships and in their careers. Their professional and personal lives blossomed after staying sober, and they enjoyed the clean living and the opportunity to change directions. Kicking the addiction was an important turning point in their lives.

Paul, whom Patty calls extremely witty, artistic, and intelligent, loved to take on new challenges. He learned to surf and golf, improved his public-speaking skills, and had started teaching a design class, all in his late 30s and early 40s. He stuck with anything new until he mastered it. When their son was born, Paul dedicated himself to the new challenge of becoming the best father he could be, fueled by the knowledge that his own father had abandoned his family when he was only five years old. Paul attended weekly meetings with other men who prioritized their role as fathers. Buzz, who was given Patty's late father's nickname, was the light of their lives. "We always thought, and still do, that Buzz was the greatest kid ever," Patty says. Ironically, Buzz was also five when Paul nearly disappeared from his family's life—although not by choice.

The Ride of His Life

On June 14, 2008, the Saturday before Father's Day, Paul, Patty, and Buzz attended a birthday party for Buzz's friend at nearby White Rock Lake in Dallas. Paul brought his bike so he could ride around the lake on his way home. Cycling was part of his commitment to better health—eating right and exercising to lose some weight and get in better shape. Paul enjoyed showing off his bike to some of the other dads at the party who were more avid cyclists. Buzz was just learning to ride a bike, and Paul patiently helped him practice that day—despite Buzz's frustration at frequently losing his balance.

After the party, just before noon, Paul left for the 10-mile ride around the lake. Patty and Buzz soon followed, planning to meet him at home. A mile from their house, traffic came to a stop. Patty saw an ambulance in the distance; she could vaguely see EMTs treating a man wearing black shorts and a white t-shirt—the same colors Paul was wearing. "I kept telling myself, 'It's not him,'" Patty says. Buzz asked Patty, "Is it Daddy?" Patty told him she was sure it wasn't. She wondered if she should run and check, but decided she couldn't leave Buzz in the car. The ambulance drove away, and traffic moved.

"I drove home as fast as I could and ran up to the front porch, but Paul wasn't there." She ran inside and checked the back porch, also finding it empty. Then the phone rang. A friend from the party saw Paul's bike on the side of the road and told Patty she suspected Paul had been in an accident. The host of the party called immediately after to confirm that Paul had indeed been struck by a car. Her husband had recognized the bike next to the road and stopped at the scene to talk to a policeman, who explained the driver had seen Paul too late while changing lanes, then panicked and slammed the clutch instead of the brakes. She offered to pick up Patty and drive her to the hospital.

Patty's friend arrived quickly—her son and a car load of birthday presents in tow—to transport Patty to Baylor Medical Center in downtown Dallas and to look after Buzz. On the way to the hospital, Patty called her sister and her mom. Her sister, who was coincidentally already downtown at a meeting, arrived at the ER first and tried to identify Paul in the emergency room, but there was so much blood, she wasn't certain of his identity. When Patty entered the ER treatment area, she couldn't see Paul's face, but recognized his body and clothing. Doctors had stitched and wrapped Paul's head. His most severe injury was to his head and brain (despite having worn a helmet). He also suffered three fractured ribs and a punctured right lung.

"I remember the doctor saying, 'I can't tell you what's going to happen. I really don't know,'" Patty says. "Then he returned and told me maybe Paul would wake up and just have a headache." All the hospital staff could say for sure was that Paul was in critical condition and unconscious, in a comatose state, and they didn't know when—or if—he would wake up. "Might Die" was listed at the top of the police accident report. That phrase seemed to sum up all that anyone knew.

As Paul stabilized and was transferred from the ER to the ICU, their friends and family arrived one or two at a time, entering a waiting room already crowded with visitors. "People had coolers, blankets, and pillows. It felt like a refugee camp that we all became a part of for two weeks," says Patty. During the following days, Paul's brother and sister-in-law, his mother, and his two sisters flew in to see him, and friends, family members, neighbors, and coworkers visited in a constant stream. "People came out of the woodwork. After the accident, it became apparent how much everyone loved him; I was bombarded by people," says Patty. "My mom tells the story of a young woman who visited and was crying while holding Paul's hand. She asked, 'Did you work with Paul?' And the woman replied, 'I used to, but he fired me.'" Even though they laughed about it, it was stories like this one that showed Patty how Paul had made an impact on so many people. Patty was amazed at the reaction from his coworkers and people whom she hardly knew, people from their past and present lives. "It was a weird juxtaposition of people. It was sad that Paul couldn't see (the outpouring of support). He would have appreciated it. His ego would have ballooned out of the room."

An Eye-Opening Experience?

In the ICU, the doctors tried to awaken Paul, pinching him and pushing his chest while calling his name. They believed Paul would wake up at any moment. To get Paul's attention, Patty played the U.S. Open Golf Tournament on TV for him—Paul's favorite sporting event. She posted updates on a blog, frequently asking friends and family to "pray for Paul to open his eyes soon." Patty says, "It gave me some power over the situation to pray and get people involved in praying."

For two weeks, doctors gave them good news and bad. Pressure on Paul's brain necessitated the insertion of a drainage tube. His vitals remained stable, and his other injuries were healing. However, scans showed a small amount of blood on the brain, and his head injuries were called "serious." Occasionally, Paul responded positively. Only days after the accident, Patty asked him to raise his finger, and Paul lifted his index finger. They hoped for more signs that Paul could hear them and would indeed wake up.

Patty's sister and a friend began researching brain injuries, only to find out how little is known. Patty decided to view this as a positive. "If they don't really know," she decided, "then they can't tell me Paul won't get better." One day, when Paul's brother was devastated by some news from the doctor, Patty told him, "But this is Paul. This is the person who will take on any challenge and will never give up!" She believed Paul would prevail, but didn't know what to expect. "We will just keep going," she said.

Patty knew that if the tables were turned and she had been the one who had been hurt, Paul would never have given up on her. He would have been her strength, and she decided that she would be strong for him, no matter what. He had been the more assertive partner, but now she had to lead. "I have to keep pushing Paul, because he would keep pushing me," she says. "It's like our philosophies in life merged. Now we've become this one thing that's moving forward."

At the end of two weeks, Paul remained unconscious. By then, all his friends and family members had visited, pleading with him to wake up. Each thought they would be the one to finally cause him to open his eyes, Patty says. "It became almost comical. They were trying to say the right words. They'd say, 'I think he squeezed my hand.'"

The day before Paul turned 44, on the last day of June, he was moved to a private room while still comatose. A few family members visited, and a happy birthday balloon was the only sign of celebration. A nephew was born in Dallas the same day, and named after Paul. Buzz hadn't realized it was his father's birthday until he heard grownups discussing his new cousin being born on his Dad's birthday. When he realized it was Paul's birthday, and that they hadn't given him a birthday party, Buzz broke down. He became livid. The seriousness of the situation suddenly became apparent to Buzz. "Why did this happen?" he repeatedly cried.

The first time Paul opened his eyes was during a sponge bath about three weeks after the accident. Nurses called Patty in to inform her that Paul's eyes were open, but that he wasn't alert. "He was by no means awake. He wasn't looking at anything," says Patty. For a while he opened one eye at a time, then both, but remained unresponsive. Patty says they learned that waking up was going to be a long process, not a momentary awakening.

One day, while Patty sat in the hospital lobby, she was approached by Paul's doctor. He informed her that he was recommending a long-term nurses' facility for Paul rather than rehabilitation and would write the discharge papers. "In a year or two, if he's still on the vent, you'll have to decide what you want to do as you evaluate his quality of life," he said. He added, "It's really not like the Terri Schiavo case. You'll have to decide what's best for him." The blunt conversation put Patty in a state of shock. She didn't know what to believe or how to react, but she didn't want to give up on Paul.

An old friend and forceful hospital attorney learned of Patty's situation and marched into the hospital to offer Patty her counsel. Standing over six feet tall in her high heels, she sat Patty down on a bench outside and listened to what the doctors had told her. "Don't sign anything!" she advised Patty, explaining that the hospital staff can't make Paul leave if she doesn't consent. "She gave me strength," said Patty. "She said, 'Don't accept what they are saying.'" She urged Patty to fight for rehabilitation services to maximize Paul's chances of regaining his well-being.

After this consultation, Patty pushed hard for the doctors to send Paul to rehabilitation. She knew Paul probably wasn't ready—it would be another month before he acknowledged his own wife—but the alternative was to provide only nursing care. Doctors reluctantly agreed to try. "He barely did enough to get in," Patty says. "It was almost a kindness."

By the fourth of July, Paul was experiencing more wakeful moments and seemed increasingly aware of his surroundings. He used his hands to feel his mouth and nose or rub his eyes and neck. He moved his legs and crossed them. Family members began to see some of Paul's mannerisms return, such as adjusting his glasses. A couple of days later, Buzz visited his dad for the first time in the hospital; Paul's brother explained the tubes and machines to him on a five-year-old level. Like any child, Buzz believed that after a time in the hospital, his dad would get better and go home. The harder part for Buzz was later, when Paul came home and wasn't yet restored to health.

Thanks to Patty's insistence, Paul was soon transferred to Baylor Specialty Hospital, to be followed by a specialist in physical medicine and rehabilitation and to receive daily respiratory, physical, occupational, and speech therapy. Although it was many weeks before he actively participated in rehab, it was this decision to pursue therapy that ultimately allowed Paul to gradually progress. Doctors explained that rather than "waking up" from a coma, Paul had to enter various levels of consciousness, and that each patient does this at his own pace, making doctors unable to determine his level of awareness at any given point.

To help stimulate his senses, Patty introduced smells, sights and sounds that were Paul's favorites. For example, Patty brought coffee, garlic, cinnamon, and peanut butter to Paul's room for him to smell. A friend made a slideshow with pictures of people whom Paul loved to display on his computer. Family played sports events for Paul to listen to and brought Paul different balls to hold. None of these items caused a strong reaction, but Patty says, "It gave me something to do rather than just sit there." She and those around Paul took note of every small improvement. "His friend would call me during the night visitation to say, 'Patty, he took his glasses off and put them back on!' We would all be celebrating. We celebrated *every* little thing." When Paul uttered his son's name, "Buzz," while observing him coloring near his bed, then reached out for him, the family was euphoric, because they knew Paul recognized his loved ones—something many brain injury victims never achieve.

In early August, Paul was moved to Baylor Rehabilitation Hospital, 45 minutes from home. There, he was diagnosed with apraxia, meaning he had the strength and will to perform certain actions, but his brain was not always able to make his body complete the tasks. Paul was also diagnosed with apraxia of speech, due to damage to the area of the brain that controls speech muscles. Even years later, Paul has an extreme speech deficit. He works with a speech therapist to continue to improve, but speaking just a few words requires tremendous effort. Only with Patty's assistance was Paul able to agree to be interviewed and answer questions for this book.

Road to Recovery

It was several months before Paul moved through all phases of consciousness. In early September, Paul recognized faces and smiled at people he knew, and even laughed at a few private jokes. Another move to a residential rehabilitation facility followed, accompanied by further progress, including Paul spelling out words on a letter board, such as, "I'm cold." This was significant, as Patty learned Paul could communicate. Not surprisingly, this was a frightening time for Paul, as he became fully aware of his predicament. Shortly after he spelled a few phrases, Patty asked, "How are you feeling?" Paul spelled, "Terrified." Patty says she began to understand how fearful Paul was, not knowing what was going on.

Paul's love for Patty and his emotional state soon poured out. For several weeks, every day when Patty visited, "It was like coming home from a war. He would grab me and sob and hold me like he didn't know where he was and he didn't know if he would see me again." It was a milestone when he could greet Patty without weeping and wondering if she would return. "It was a gradual increase in clarity—and he still gets clarity now from time to time," Patty says, now three years after the accident.

The following months were like putting pieces of a puzzle together. Paul always knew he and Patty were a couple, but he once spelled out "Will you marry me?" and Patty had to remind him, "I already did!" There were times when Paul would ask about deceased relatives. He frequently asked about his twin brother, a military man who had drowned in a rafting accident with friends when he was only 18. "I would have to tell Paul (his brother) had died, and he would be devastated," said Patty. Then Paul would forget, and she'd have to remind him. He asked to speak to Patty's father, who had died a year before Buzz was born. Patty had to explain his passing as well. "He was so sad. It was like hearing it for the first time."

Patty was relieved that Paul's sense of humor and his personality were intact, although she says he is sort of a "lighter version" of the Paul prior to the accident. "He was so intense, and he still is intense about many things, but he used to worry a lot and his mind raced about how he would accomplish things. Now I think he's still a determined person, but he doesn't worry about as much, except about basics like walking and talking better and being the best dad for Buzz." Paul remains funny, determined, and artistic.

Despite his long road to healing, Patty is grateful that Paul pulled through—for her sake and for Buzz's. Paul has given love and gratitude to Patty for her constant support, even if he can't always express it in words. Of their relationship, Patty says, "It just feels like it was meant to be, even more so (than prior to the accident). I have a stronger belief that this is where I was meant to be and that we were meant to be together. I think he feels it even more. He does depend on me."

Patty says Buzz was the positive force that kept Paul and Patty motivated during difficult weeks and months. Buzz made them laugh or smile on days they felt like giving up, and continues to motivate them to work harder so he can have an active father in his life. Their extended family also acted as a buoy that kept them both from drowning in fear and sorrow. Patty says the accident catapulted her and Paul to a new life, "but family and friends were there to catch us, gently place us on the ground, and have helped clear our pathway as much as possible."

Paul and Patty's family members helped in many concrete ways —providing meals, caring for Buzz for weeks at a time, organizing all of their finances and hospital bills, and more. "I can't imagine having this happen and not having a family to pitch in. It was such a blessing," Patty says, her voice cracking. Even now, her siblings help her take Paul to events, such as Buzz's ball games, so Paul can stand and cheer.

Friends not only provided emotional assistance, they also held fund raisers to assist with medical bills. A golf outing called Jerde's Cup raised $60,000, which paid for medical care. Patty had been laid off from her job at the time of the accident, but was later recalled and now works from home most days, with an accommodating employer and supportive coworkers. Paul also receives disability, and random people have sent Paul and Patty money to help, demonstrating widespread generosity. Having to worry about finances, particularly during the first year, would have been overwhelming, says Patty. The experience has altered their view of the community—as being more expansive and supportive than they previously realized.

Homeward Bound

Paul's memory was significantly restored, although he occasionally experiences some confusion about events just prior to and after the accident. He has excellent recollection of people, names, and events from his past. Paul learned to stand and to walk somewhat with the help of a specialized walker, although his right side was significantly impaired and his balance is unstable. (He was right-handed and has little use of his right arm or hand.) He re-learned how to use a computer but faces some frustration due to the apraxia. He still enjoys painting; he and Buzz often brush away on side-by-side canvasses.

In November of 2008, technology greatly enhanced Paul's ability to communicate. He received a DynaVox, a touch-screen device that uses a keyboard, word prediction, and voice activation to articulate phrases for him. While it does not take the place of speech therapy, it allowed Paul to join conversations and communicate significantly better with Patty and others. It requires some patience for those around him, who must slow the conversation to allow him to participate. Paul's sense of humor and quick wit are still with him, although it's slower to come out with the DynaVox.

As Buzz's reading continues to improve, the DynaVox is helping Paul and Buzz communicate better. The frustration between them is sometimes palpable when each of them doesn't feel they can speak and be heard in a manner in which they used to communicate. However, they enjoy moments of strong connection, such as when Buzz and Paul play tug-of-war during physical-therapy exercises or when they get in the swimming pool together—Paul with his life vest and belt on, and Buzz able to climb on his Dad like the old days. And there is connection in their eyes, in their touches. Buzz talks to a therapist about his feelings and struggles, as his life has also significantly changed since Paul's accident.

In December of 2008—about six months after the accident—Paul was able to move back home, although with some difficulty. Their house had to be modified to accommodate his needs, with a walk-in shower and enlarged bathroom. Paul's sister temporarily moved to Dallas to help Patty care for Buzz and Paul. Patty said she had to learn how to shower and shave for Paul. "It made my knees weak to shave him." She searched *YouTube* for how-to videos on shaving. (Later, he learned to use an electric razor.) In addition to self-care, they managed his medications; he was treated for digestive problems due to sitting all day, and given an antidepressant and anti-anxiety medication, as well as medications to help his memory and focus.

Patty's new role as caregiver, rather than simply wife, certainly changed their relationship. "It's hard to describe. I still feel like we're a team. This is our new journey; it just changed from being everyday life," Patty says. "We're faced with different challenges, but we're still facing it and I depend on him to keep working every day." Patty does not lament her role as a constant caregiver, and she has no regrets about where she ended up in life. "I'd choose the same path, because it brought me to Paul and Buzz." She is thankful for every choice that led her to where she is, and appreciates that they are surrounded by family members.

Patty understandably experiences some sadness regarding Paul's loss of abilities, but the grieving comes in small spurts, not one long process. Patty and Paul have little time for grieving, as they are focused on Paul's improvement.

While Patty had to make all the family and health decisions following the accident, she says they have evolved to a partnership, discussing challenges and figuring things out together, from purchases to treatments to how to care for Buzz. Patty allows that the situation is totally different than she would have ever imagined, but she remains positive about her circumstances. Rather than focusing on what they have lost, she speaks of how far they have come.

Positive attitude determines much in the way of success in a tumultuous situation. How does Patty explain her ability to remain positive? "We're here and we're faced with this. We can either lock the door and stay home, or we can try as much as we can." She has always told Paul he would do something extraordinary with his life. She had always believed it, but wasn't sure what his accomplishment would be. She reminds Paul that he will still have extraordinary accomplishments. She finds other champions to encourage them, sometimes strangers who are taken by Paul's charisma, which he still conveys. "They see something in Paul and want to be a part of it," Patty says.

Patty says prior to the accident, her life and Paul's were connected, but parallel, with a lot of activity and occasional intersections. The accident brought them to a new level of closeness. "We've been through things that are indescribable," she says. "Our lives took a different turn. We're doing this together."

"We always had a strong marriage, but (the accident) definitely unified us. We're just one now," Patty says. But there is a downside to that constant togetherness. "Sometimes it can be overwhelming. In some ways, I liked being two separate people with two separate lives. It's important that we have our independence." To that end, she encourages Paul to maintain his involvement in his men's group, and she has realized her need to have some time to herself as well. Any marriage must have a balance of independence and dependence, but because of Paul's physical dependence, it's even more important for the Jerdes to create opportunities for independence from one another.

"Everyone says, 'Take time for yourself,' but no one has told me quite how to do that," says Patty, who shuttles Paul to therapy appointments while working and caring for Buzz. She would like to run more, and Paul wants her to take care of herself, but for a long time she felt guilty about the idea of running when Paul couldn't even walk. Now she views it as a stress-reliever.

Unable to leave Buzz and Paul alone for more than a brief period, Patty needs outside help any time she wishes to leave the house, but she believes that will improve as Paul becomes more independent and as Buzz gets older. (He is nine now.) Patty also turns to her sisters when she feels stress. "I'll just call and say we had a bad morning, and they listen." Paul's family visits every couple of months to give Patty a break from her caregiver responsibilities. And she tries to arrange lunch with a friend every month or two. "It feels normal, like what I used to do," Patty says.

In addition to maintaining a positive attitude regarding Paul's therapy, Patty says networking and researching new breakthroughs is also helpful. "There are a lot of opportunities out there. Do not give up," she advises anyone who has a spouse with a medical condition. She says friends and family help them stay abreast of medical advancements and treatments, such as equine (horse) or water therapy. She likes to hear about other success stories, but she recognizes that they are in uncharted territory. Patty has learned to trust her gut and follow her instincts. "No one is me. Even the doctors don't have a spouse with a brain injury," she says. "They can only tell you what they think."

Patty says people approach her frequently and say, "I couldn't do that," of her commitment to her husband. While Paul was still comatose, a hospital visitor told Patty he recalled a friend with a brain injury whose wife left him after the accident; the man later improved and remarried. Patty is surprised people relay this kind of story, and she isn't sure why some people give up so easily. Patty insists most people would do exactly what she is doing, and that her efforts aren't so extraordinary. "You would just do it. It's not like I ever thought of not doing it. It became what our life is, just like anything else, and became a part of us. If you're already committed to the relationship, I don't think it would change you. It makes you rise to the challenge."

Patty's resolve may offer hope to spouses facing seemingly too-difficult fates—whether caring for a spouse with a terminal illness, dementia, or a long-term disability. It may not be what you imagined, but it's certainly in the realm of "for better or for worse." Patty provides a positive model for gracefully and lovingly moving on with her family intact.

Patty expects their life to be constantly changing as Paul's abilities improve. They continue to stimulate his brain with new experiences and therapies. She also wants the accident to have a positive impact on their son. "I try to look to the future, and I want Buzz to be a better person because of all this. How we'll get there, I don't know—but I know we'll stay a strong family." Paul remains committed to his therapy and becoming the best father he can be. The men's group in which he had become involved continues to support Paul, taking him to rehab appointments and driving him to their meetings.

Paul and Patty still dream of their future, playing golf and going out to eat with friends. Their long-term goal is to take a trip to New York to watch the U.S. Open Tennis Tournament at night, something they've always wanted to do. Sometimes Patty will remind Paul of their goal. "We have so much to do. We have to get to the U.S. Open," she'll tell him. "Yeah!" he responds, and keeps working.

The Jerdes demonstrate that marriage often follows the unplanned route. Accidents and emergencies occur without warning, and the resulting adversity changes us—sometimes for the better and sometimes not. Paul and Patty have benefited from the love and support of their community, which improved their view of the outside world. They allowed an accident to crystallize their marriage, making it more unified and solid than before. Far from being a marriage where each partner is concerned primarily with his or her own needs, they have experienced a tested but determined marriage partnership. The sacrifice may be more one-sided, but the hard work and gratitude flow both ways.

As of late 2011, Paul continues to participate in ongoing speech, occupational and physical therapy, making improvements "at a snail's pace." Patty says they celebrate small victories, such as when Paul can speak a complete sentence without his iPad (which has become a useful tool), letter board or other device. While he cannot yet walk alone, he continues to make small advances there as well. "Neither of us will give up until he gets there," Patty says.

"I still feel so much love for Paul and feel so strongly about what we're going through. Sometimes I think that even though this is a tragedy, it has made our lives extraordinary. It's something that other people won't go through. It's a whole different life experience."

Lesson:

Happiness is not the goal of marriage. However, it's often a wonderful byproduct of deep and lasting love.

CHAPTER 12:

OVERCOMING DARK DAYS

Seventeen-year-old John "Jack" McCannon met 14-year-old Eileen King in 1936 during the bleak days of the Great Depression. Both were students at Catholic Central High School in Fort Madison, Iowa, a small town on the banks of the Mississippi River. He played basketball, and she was a cheerleader. Jack was taken by how beautiful and fun Eileen was. She was impressed by his charm. "He just got my dander up," she says. He was and still is quite a conversationalist.

Although the energetic couple enjoyed sports, including golf, tennis, and bowling, the one thing that really took their minds off of the tough times was dancing. With no television, teens frequently held dances. Jack and Eileen loved to dance, especially the jitterbug. They danced well together and often. Even during lunch hour at school, they danced in the auditorium to the record player. They danced into each other's hearts, despite the fact that Eileen's mother, Amelia, didn't approve of Jack—at least at first.

Jack was from the wrong part of town, and his family didn't have much money. Eileen's family, on the other hand, had money —or at least, they did before the Depression. Eileen's father, John, had owned a bank in West Point, Iowa, until an employee embezzled money; there was no FDIC to protect banks back then, and he lost everything. As a result, when Eileen was in fifth grade, her family was forced to relocate to Fort Madison, where her father became a guard at the state prison. Her mother, Amelia, was a hat maker and seamstress; she sewed beautiful dresses for Eileen to wear to all the big dances. Naturally, Eileen's parents wanted her to marry into a "respectable" family.

Although her parents no doubt suffered due to their changing fortunes, Eileen herself wasn't aware of the huge financial changes. They had all the basics, and Eileen didn't miss what they didn't have. Apart from the loss of a brother, who died at age seven from infantile paralysis (loss of children from illness was much more common then; the McCannons recall some families losing five children in one year), Eileen describes her childhood as lovely and uneventful.

Jack's childhood, however, was anything but lovely. By age 17, he had endured a lifetime's worth of struggles. His father abandoned his family—relocating to Kansas City, where he later remarried— when Jack was only seven years old. Alone with three children and no support during a period that saw record levels of unemployment, Jack's mother, Pauline, found work at Sheaffer Pen factory as a grinder. "My mother worked all day in the factory grinding pens. Her hands were full of cuts and jabs from the pens," Jack explains. Even so, she was unable to make ends meet, making $3 a day, three days a week. Jack and his sister, Lorraine, were sent to live with their maternal grandmother across town, while his mother and brother, Harry Jr., moved in with his mother's sister. With no car, the divided family saw little of each other.

Also living with Jack's grandmother were several aunts and uncles. There was always a long list of chores to do, such as feeding the chickens. Birthdays passed unnoticed; there was simply no money for extras. The children didn't know what candy was. Jack and his brother worked on a farm during the summers to help support the family. Later, he worked at his uncle's grocery store. Living above a grocery store nearly killed him. Jack became blind with typhoid fever, which was traced to contaminated water that came from a nearby well. Luckily, the condition—like the kidney disease from which he suffered that flared up from time to time—was treatable, and he returned to health. But as difficult as it was, the hardship Jack endured during his youth served to prepare him for even more grueling days ahead, and helped him appreciate the simple joys in life.

A Lifeline during War

After graduating from high school in 1938, Jack landed a good job with the railroad and continued to date Eileen on and off. The times they were "off" were mostly because Eileen's mother wanted her to date other people. Jack says he always knew Eileen was "the one" for him. Eileen felt the same way, but added that she was only 14 when she and Jack had started dating. They had the occasional fight, and her mother tried to break them up. "She would have picked a guy with a car and money who lived in a nice house," Eileen explains, but the two kept finding each other. "It hurt me quite a bit that she was seeing others. It was hard for me to compete, with no car and little money," Jack shares. "I couldn't blame her mother for wanting her to be with someone who had more to offer financially," concedes Jack. "But (Eileen) chose me."

Once he had a good job, life was finally improving for Jack. But on December 7, 1941, Pearl Harbor was attacked. Suddenly, all young men were called to military service to support World War II. Jack joined the Navy so he could choose a post instead of being drafted. By this time, Jack and Eileen had fallen deeper in love, and became engaged despite their unknown futures and the start of the war.

Jack went to boot camp, where he saw many soldiers weeping over being sent to war and away from their families. "They missed home," Jack explains. They weren't used to being treated like (soldiers). Their bodies weren't in shape for calisthenics and climbing over walls. That was pickins' for me. I was skin and bones, lean and mean. It was no problem for me to do it." He continues, "One guy was upset because he wasn't allowed to wipe his running nose when he marched." Jack and his fellow trainees slept in hammocks connected to posts. They were uncomfortable, and sometimes soldiers fell out. To Jack, though, it was no big deal, you just got back up. "I had pretty much been on my own since I was about 11, so nothing surprised me," Jack says. Having already been hardened to tough life and hard work, Jack did not consider his circumstances bleak.

At boot camp, the men were tested on various skills to determine where they could best help the war effort. Jack says he tested well on all of the skills except mechanics. He did especially well on radio skills, including International Code (similar to Morse code), so he was chosen for this area of training. Following boot camp, the military sent him to the University of Idaho to radio school. "I learned dots and dashes from 8 to 5, then had dinner and was back in class from 6 to 9 at night," says Jack. "We took a nine-month course in three months." He was then chosen to go to Naval Intelligence School in Seattle. Jack took a vow of secrecy back then, and still doesn't like to share much detail about his training, but it certainly helped in the war.

Since Jack thought he would be in Seattle for a while at the Naval Intelligence School, he and Eileen set a wedding date and made preparations for Eileen to travel to Seattle for the ceremony. But Jack was unexpectedly shipped out early, on Christmas Day of 1942, before they could tie the knot. Jack soon landed at Pearl Harbor, where the destruction wrought by the attack the year prior was still very evident. Many destroyed ships, including the U.S.S. Oklahoma, were still sticking out of the water.

Jack and Eileen didn't see each other at all from May of 1942 to June of 1945. Jack was stationed in the Pacific—primarily on Oahu but moving every 10 months or so to other islands—where he intercepted enemy communications. (Jack narrowly escaped death when a tidal wave swamped Palmira Island, where he was stationed at the time; he waded for a spell in the water, but emerged unhurt.) Jack's job, along with other U.S. intelligence officers elsewhere in the region, was to use triangulation to pinpoint the enemy's location to within 50 miles so that they could be captured or attacked. (Jack received multiple commendations from the Navy, which said his work crushed two enemy fleets, enabling their surrenders. According to one commendation, he also "helped bring the U.S. land-based airpower within bombing range of the enemy.")

During those three lonely years, Eileen wrote a letter to Jack every single day. "Those letters meant *everything* to me," Jack says now. "I was out there so long I wondered if home was real." Eileen's chatty letters were a lifeline—his link to home, to reality. In addition to keeping him updated on family and local Fort Madison news, the letters, which he often received in batches of three or four at a time due to delivery delays, served to fuel their love. He wrote back a couple times a week as he was able.

Life wasn't easy back home, with many items, such as meat, stockings and shoes, being rationed. For her part, Eileen kept busy. After she finished high school, she took an office job working at the same Sheaffer Pen factory where Jack's mother, sister, and brother worked. Since she worked in the bookkeeping department, she didn't work closely with his family members, "but we always got along well," she says. She spent time with her girlfriends, and they all wrote letters to soldiers they knew to try to keep their spirits up.

Most of the men were at war, so there was little temptation to date. Eileen worried incessantly about Jack and all the other soldiers she knew. She prayed, waited and wrote letters. She looked for clues in his letters to find out how he was doing or where he was. "Once, he mentioned Palmira, Missouri, in a letter. So I knew he was on Palmira Island," Eileen said. She tried to write notes that were short and upbeat, giving him updates on the community. She couldn't wait for Jack and his fellow soldiers to return home.

After three long years of military service abroad, Jack returned to the U.S. in late June of 1945. On July 3, Jack and Eileen were married at long last in their hometown of Fort

Madison. They had waited years for this moment, and not even the scorching heat—the temperature approached 110 degrees—could mar the day. Jack, weighing 152 pounds with a 29-inch waist, was terribly handsome in his blues uniform, and Eileen, wearing a long dress and veil and carrying a mixed bouquet of flowers, was so beautiful she could have picked any man. They were ready to start their lives together. "I was very excited. I could hardly wait after all that time," Eileen says.

Not many men were present at Saint Mary's Church for their wedding, since most were still away at war, but all of Eileen's girlfriends were there. "Only one male friend was there," says Eileen, "and he had been deferred for health reasons." Jack's and Eileen's families came, as well as Eileen's coworkers at Scheaffer. Eileen's parents had gotten to know Jack and accepted him by then, and were pleased about the wedding. Jack thinks a turning point may have been while he was away and Navy officers came back to his hometown to interview everyone he ever met because of the job for which he was being chosen.

Following the wedding and a brief honeymoon in Iowa, Jack and Eileen moved to San Diego, where Jack, who was still in the Navy, was stationed. Eileen performed office work at the base on a part-time basis. Jack's schedule—working one day on and one day off—allowed plenty of time for fun excursions to Mexico and Malibu, which they made in a Model T Ford they bought for one hundred dollars. "Every time we went up a hill," Jack recalls with a laugh, "the radiator shot water in the air."

Jack was discharged in October of 1945, after the war ended. Although Jack and Eileen had enjoyed San Diego, Jack had no intention of making a career in the military. And while he had a chance to study meteorology in California under the G.I. Bill, he was eager to get back home, back to "normal." He had been on his own from a young age and didn't want to put his life on hold for another four years. Jack explains, "Being brought up in the Depression, we were raised to feel the job is the most important thing. I knew I had a good one waiting for me."

A New Start Back Home

For Jack, "back to normal" meant back to work at the railroad, where he served as a switchman, brakeman, conductor, and engine foreman. And in a short time, Jack and Eileen had begun a family, with their first son, John, arriving in 1947. Around the same time, Eileen's parents suffered a financial setback and needed money to buy a house. Jack loaned them his entire life savings, $2,700 (equivalent to about ten times as much today), which he had accrued during the war; Eileen's parents used it to help purchase a house across the street. "They needed the money, and we had it," says Jack. Besides, he adds, "we weren't used to having money, so it wasn't that hard to give it. My wife asked me to do it, and I did it. As I look back on it now, I can't believe it. When I was growing up I had absolutely nothing. For four years, I saved all my earnings."

Later that same year, Eileen's youngest sister, Nancy, who was then in the eighth grade, came home from school one day to find the oven on and their mother dead on the floor. "My mother was absentminded," Eileen recalls. "She probably forgot the stove was on, and was overcome by the gas." After that, Eileen and Jack took Eileen's father and her two sisters, Patricia and Nancy, into their home—a three-bedroom apartment. Needless to say, quarters were tight.

Now, in addition to the baby, Eileen was taking care of two teenage girls and two grown men. And her burden grew along with their family: In 1950, daughter Kathy was born, followed by Mark in 1953 (the year Eileen's father passed away) and Beth in 1956. (To accommodate their expanding brood, Jack and Eileen moved to a larger house with a park nearby.) But Eileen embraced her role, which seemed to come to her naturally, and which she performed without complaint—even though Jack, who frequently calls her "Saint Eileen," worked the 2:30 a.m. to 10:30 a.m. shift, after which he often played golf or poker. Jack confesses that Eileen did most of the child rearing; "I don't know how she put up with me," he says. Despite all the work, Eileen doesn't remember things as being tough. "I was more of a homebody," Eileen explains, and says she enjoyed some alone time to read books. "I've loved reading books since I was a child." She adds, "We hardly ever had any cross words in our marriage," she says. The priest who married us told us to never go to sleep mad. We hardly ever get mad (at one another)."

For Jack, poker wasn't just a hobby—it was like a second job. He played twice a week for 45 years with good success, and parlayed his winnings into the stock market. Eileen didn't take issue with Jack's poker playing—except for one time, when he was arrested for gambling and it was listed in the paper. When it was time to retire from his "regular job", Jack continued to play poker for supplemental income until 1994, when the steamboat casinos came to his town along the Mississippi River. Many of his poker friends started to play on the boats, but he quit playing, realizing his odds of success substantially declined. And, knowing the odds as well as he does, he doesn't enjoy other forms of gambling. "I wouldn't waste the money," he says. Jack became very knowledgeable about the stock market and invested his earnings and winnings well. "She gave me free reign, but I did a pretty good job," says Jack. In addition to supporting the family financially, Jack did so in other important ways—for example, attending the kids' important events, such as baseball and basketball games. And he has always done the grocery shopping; Eileen is a great cook and enjoys preparing meals.

A Great Loss

The McCannons hardly blinked when Jack had a malignant growth removed from his kidney in 1975; after all, he was strong and healthy. Jack, even in his 90s, is still mowing the lawn. What shook them to the core was when their son, Mark, then 46 and single, was diagnosed with lung cancer in 1999. The doctor gave Mark—their vibrant, maverick son, a Clint Eastwood lookalike—18 months to live. They had just traveled to the Masters Golf Tournament together (at Mark's suggestion) a couple of days before Mark received the news.

Mark, who lived in Portland, Oregon, initially underwent chemotherapy and radiation on his own, but finally agreed to return to Fort Madison at his parents' urging in September of the same year. He got an apartment near Jack and Eileen's home. Mark visited often for dinner, and Jack and Mark frequently played golf together for the five weeks Mark was feeling well. And although Mark had sometimes clashed with his dad growing up—"He was a chip off the old block," Eileen explains—he and his dad enjoyed the opportunity to truly reconnect. Sadly, though, Mark's treatment was not successful. About seven months after his diagnosis, in November of 1999, he stopped eating, and he felt his body shutting down. He didn't want his mother and father to see him lying in bed, wasting away, kept alive with tubes; after leaving a note asking police not to wake his parents until morning so as not to disturb their sleep, he shot himself.

The McCannons missed Mark terribly. "We had so much in common," says Jack. "We talked about the stock market, golf tournaments—anything." And like his dad, Mark also worked with the railroads—Santa Fe and Amtrak. Many of Mark's friends still visit Jack and Eileen, bringing fresh tomatoes or farm eggs. They tell Jack that Mark frequently passed along his father's wisdom, and that they had benefited from Jack's advice over the years. "Life's amazing," muses Jack. "I didn't think he had any respect for me back then. But he talked about me all the time." And while the death of a child stresses many marriages, Jack and Eileen supported each other in their grief. "We got through it together," they say.

The Good Times

The McCannons have experienced sorrows and trials during their 60-plus years of marriage, but with patience, they have seen what comes on the other side. "Neither of us has ever thought of not continuing in our marriage," they say. They attribute growing up in the Great Depression with making them strong; they learned early the importance of working hard and carried that lesson into the rest of their lives—including their marriage.

Each of them was comfortable in their respective roles. They agree that they had realistic expectations of one another, and a love that went well beyond the surface. They had a good balance of enjoying separate activities, while not letting anything come between them. "We are private people. We have always been joined at the hip, and nobody gets in—not even our kids," says Jack. "We're so dependent on each other. I make sure she gets her oxygen (she now has some breathing problems). She looks after me, too. I handle the finances, and she balances the checkbook." Eileen says the relationship they now enjoy after 60 years together reminds her of her grandparents'. "He died before she did, and in two weeks, she also died. She wasn't sick; she just didn't want to go on without him. It's the companionship; it is a treasure for me, especially now that so many of our friends have died."

Their commitment to each other, to their family, and to hard work has led to great satisfaction in their later years. Their secret, they say, is taking things one day at a time, and never trying to impress others. They work together, with a lot of give and take, and they treat each other well. "We've never been mean to each other," they say. And although Jack and Eileen didn't pepper their children with advice about love and marriage, both say they tried to model a strong marriage for them. "They saw the way we lived and learned from our example," notes Jack. The big lessons they communicate: "Love is important. Respect is even more so. If you don't have that, you have nothing. Respect each other's point of view. Give and take, and don't smother each other." Jack adds that their faith has helped sustain them. "We both have a very deep faith, and that was really helpful through the war, too. Our faith has been there, no matter what."

Although Jack sometimes regrets that he didn't take advantage of the G.I. Bill, Eileen says she is "perfectly happy" with the way things turned out. (However, they both do wish that they had kept Jack's uniform and the more than 1,000 letters she wrote during the war.) Besides, their children received the gift of education, starting with Catholic school and most going on to college. (Jack doesn't take credit; he notes that their kids worked hard to help pay for their schooling.) And their eight grandchildren have been remarkably successful, becoming a pediatric nurse, a usability aeronautics engineer, an architectural engineer, an assistant basketball coach, an agricultural product research specialist, an ER nurse who works in medical forensics, a bank loan officer, and a college student. "They are strong and educated," says Jack. "We are so proud, because neither of us went to college."

When the McCannon's last child left home, Jack put his arm around Eileen and said, "It's just you and me the rest of the way." Even still, Jack tears up when he recalls that special milestone moment. They have certainly enjoyed their empty-nest years. Eileen, who started working part-time at a bank located half a block from their home when their oldest child was grown, retired in 1979 at age 57 and Jack, then 60, retired the same year—neither with any intention of slowing down. Devoted Catholics, both still attend daily Mass. Sports have also been a big focus; both Jack and Eileen bowled well into their 80s, played golf, and spent three months each year in Rio Grand Valley playing team tennis. These days, they remain active socially, playing cards—especially bridge—with friends. Jack plays pool and golf a couple times a week. Both say time spent apart with friends has been good for their marriage. "We go our own way. You need some space," they agree.

The Only Constant is Change

The McCannons and others of their generation have experienced more changes than perhaps any other in U.S. history. They went from living in homes with a single light bulb to iPods and the Internet, from horses and buggies to supersonic jets. When they were married, $5,000 bought a great house; now, a new car costs five times as much. "It kills me to pay $1.75 for a cup of coffee, jokes Jack. He also worries about the effects of food prices in developing countries.

The social changes that have occurred during their lives have likewise been dramatic—and meaningful. Although Jack and Eileen question the influence of television and other media on today's children, they say some social changes have been much needed. For example, when they were young, a woman who became pregnant out of wedlock was sometimes disowned, sent away, or treated horribly —even by her own family. "That was cruel," they agree. On the other hand, they worry the pendulum has swung too far in the other direction, with so many teens having sex in high school.

Another change the McCannons have observed relates to views on marriage. "In our generation, we took marriage for granted," they say. They observe that today's women are strong and independent and think they don't need marriage. And they note that while decades ago, society looked down on women who lived with a man out of wedlock, today women can decide what kind of life they want to live without that moral pressure. But while they acknowledge that it's a different world, they assert that the institution is still important to them.

What hasn't changed in all the decades Jack and Eileen have been together is their dedication to one another and to their marriage, their commitment to family, and their respect and love. Their long-lasting marriage has given each of them tremendous joy and left their family a great legacy.

While Jack and Eileen will always remember how well they danced together in their younger years, they explain that age has gotten in the way of dancing. Jack tried to take Eileen out on the dance floor at two recent grandchildren's wedding receptions. "Just last year, she said she couldn't do it anymore," Jack says. So instead, they sit on the couch and happily watch *Dancing with the Stars* together. "We can always pick the winners," they say.

Lessons Learned

I learned many lessons when interviewing these twelve exceptional couples and studying their lives, but the following twelve lessons stood out:

1. Never take your life, health or sobriety for granted. Steer clear of addictions.
2. Focus on your strengths, not your sorrows.
3. Forgiveness is a gift for the giver and the receiver.
4. Love is not enough to make a marriage work; it takes commitment and hard work.
5. Live each day with gratitude, and infuse your marriage with it.
6. Have each other's back. Be a team. Become one.
7. Our spouse cannot be our true source of joy.
8. The marriage should be a higher priority than the children or the inability to bear children.
9. Love is sacrificial; create a cycle of giving.
10. Things don't always (or even usually) go as planned.
11. Adversity is not a killer—it can be a strengthener.
12. Happiness is not the goal of marriage. However, it is often a wonderful byproduct of deep and lasting love.

Share your lessons with those you love or at www.LoriDLowe.com.

ACKNOWLEDGEMENTS

I offer a heartfelt thanks to the many individuals who helped me on the journey from the spark of an idea to a completed book. The early and lasting encouragement from both my husband, Ming, and from my dear friend and creative genius, Sharron Wright, have meant so much to me. They kept me moving forward each time I faced obstacles or frustration.

I am most appreciative of the twelve couples who each gave me many hours of their time and were giving in spirit; thank you so much for your generosity. Your marriages are an inspiration, and you demonstrate what true marriage should be.

When literary agent Uwe Stender, PhD, of TriadaUS Literary Agency, added his interest to the book, it helped me believe the project could positively impact many marriages. I appreciate his advice and encouragement. I'm also grateful for the editorial guidance of Kate Shoup.

Thanks to my parents, siblings and grandmother for their ongoing support of me and my writing. I can't even begin to list all the friends who have nudged me along and expressed their support and interest. A special note of gratitude to my two children for their patience as I spent many hours working on interviews, writing, editing, researching and publishing. I could not have succeeded in this endeavor without all of your love and faith in me.

Words do not seem adequate to express my deep appreciation to you all.

ABOUT THE AUTHOR

Lori D. Lowe has a master's degree in journalism from Indiana University and is a writer and communications consultant. She researches marriage trends and frequently interviews industry experts and happily married couples. Lori, a GenXer and child of divorce, lives with her husband and two children in Indianapolis. She created the popular marriage blog, MarriageGems.com in 2008, which provides hundreds of free research-based marriage tips. Lori is a newspaper columnist, a contributing writer for the local NBC affiliate, and a frequent contributor for the Coalition for Divorce Reform. In 2010, she received the top nonfiction writing award given by the Midwest Writers Workshop. Share your story, or learn more about Lori at www.LoriDLowe.com. Read the blog, or subscribe to have marriage tips emailed to you at www.MarriageGems.com.